Stanford University
Stanford, California

Written by Ian Spiro

*Edited by Adam Burns, Kevan Gray, Allison Drash,
Kimberly Moore, and Jonathan Skindzier*

Layout by Alissa Garcia

*Additional contributions by Omid Gohari,
Christina Koshzow, Christopher Mason, Joey Rahimi,
and Luke Skurman*

ISBN # 1-59658-123-9
ISSN # 1552-0684
© Copyright 2005 College Prowler
All Rights Reserved
Printed in the U.S.A.
www.collegeprowler.com

Last updated on 9/23/05

Special thanks to: Babs Carryer, Andy Hannah, LaunchCyte, Tim O'Brien, Bob Sehlinger, Thomas Emerson, Andrew Skurman, Barbara Skurman, Bert Mann, Dave Lehman, Daniel Fayock, Chris Babyak, The Donald H. Jones Center for Entrepreneurship, Terry Slease, Jerry McGinnis, Bill Ecenberger, Idie McGinty, Kyle Russell, Jacque Zaremba, Larry Winderbaum, Roland Allen, Jon Reider, Team Evankovich, Lauren Varacalli, Abu Noaman, Mark Exler, Daniel Steinmeyer, Jared Cohon, Gabriela Oates, David Koegler, and Glen Meakem.

Bounce-Back Team: Carrie Kemper, Fred Akalin, and Simon Hu

College Prowler®
5001 Baum Blvd.
Suite 750
Pittsburgh, PA 15213

Phone: 1-800-290-2682
Fax: 1-800-772-4972
E-mail: info@collegeprowler.com
Web site: www.collegeprowler.com

Welcome to College Prowler®

During the writing of College Prowler's guidebooks, we felt it was critical that our content was unbiased and unaffiliated with any college or university. We think it's important that our readers get honest information and a realistic impression of the student opinions on any campus—that's why if any aspect of a particular school is terrible, we (unlike a campus brochure) intend to publish it. While we do keep an eye out for the occasional extremist—the cheerleader or the cynic—we take pride in letting the students tell it like it is. We strive to create a book that's as representative as possible of each particular campus. Our books cover both the good and the bad, and whether the survey responses point to recurring trends or a variation in opinion, these sentiments are directly and proportionally expressed through our guides.

College Prowler guidebooks are in the hands of students throughout the entire process of their creation. Because you can't make student-written guides without the students, we have students at each campus who help write, randomly survey their peers, edit, layout, and perform accuracy checks on every book that we publish. From the very beginning, student writers gather the most up-to-date stats, facts, and inside information on their colleges. They fill each section with student quotes and summarize the findings in editorial reviews. In addition, each school receives a collection of letter grades (A through F) that reflect student opinion and help to represent contentment, prominence, or satisfaction for each of our 20 specific categories. Just as in grade school, the higher the mark the more content, more prominent, or more satisfied the students are with the particular category.

Once a book is written, additional students serve as editors and check for accuracy even more extensively. Our bounce-back team—a group of randomly selected students who have no involvement with the project—are asked to read over the material in order to help ensure that the book accurately expresses every aspect of the university and its students. This same process is applied to the 200-plus schools College Prowler currently covers. Each book is the result of endless student contributions, hundreds of pages of research and writing, and countless hours of hard work. All of this has led to the creation of a student information network that stretches across the nation to every school that we cover. It's no easy accomplishment, but it's the reason that our guides are such a great resource.

When reading our books and looking at our grades, keep in mind that every college is different and that the students who make up each school are not uniform—as a result, it is important to assess schools on a case-by-case basis. Because it's impossible to summarize an entire school with a single number or description, each book provides a dialogue, not a decision, that's made up of 20 different topics and hundreds of student quotes. In the end, we hope that this guide will serve as a valuable tool in your college selection process. Enjoy!

OMID GOHARI ◯ CHRISTINA KOSHZOW ◯ CHRIS MASON ◯ JOEY RAHIMI ◯ LUKE SKURMAN ◯
The College Prowler Team

Table of Contents

Introduction from the Author

When I started looking at colleges, I was a greasy-faced teenager in Upstate New York with a penchant for computer programming and the German language. I took honors and AP classes at my medium-sized suburban public high school, and I was engaged in that timeless and honorable process of getting into college. It was a fairly haphazard procedure for me. I knew roughly what I wanted to study, but didn't know what I wanted in a university. Ultimately, I found myself with just a few options for schools to attend. I lucked out in that the school I picked worked out to be a good match for me. I don't know how things would be if I ended up somewhere that didn't fit my personality or academic style; but I suggest you do what you can to avoid a negative outcome. By reading this book, it seems you are already taking a step in the right direction.

Back in high school, when I heard the word "Stanford," my first thoughts were of academic elitism, basketball, palm trees, and sunny skies. I've come to find out that it's much more complicated than that. Now when I hear the word "Stanford," I shudder as several thousand memories are triggered in my brain: Math 51 problem sets and Domino's pizza at 2 a.m., a social epiphany on my freshman ski trip in Lake Tahoe, impersonating and being impersonated by friends on Instant Messenger, eating Currywurst in Berlin, driving my shoddy automobile around in San Francisco, pulling three consecutive all-nighters during Dead Week . . . and these are just a few of the things that come to mind.

Stanford has been a mixed bag—mostly good, but also a bit crappy and unsatisfying. The weather is great, but I don't have much time to get out and appreciate it. A lot of the students are interesting and worth meeting, but the ones in my classes tend to be socially insane. Most of us are talented and smart, but we're also overcommitted and habitually unpunctual. But don't give up on Stanford just yet. If your college experience seems to end up absolutely perfect, I would contend that there's actually something wrong with you. So read on, and figure out what's good and what's mediocre about this place. If you like what you read, consider applying, visiting, or even attending. Good luck, and I hope you enjoy the book.

Ian Spiro, Author
Stanford University

By the Numbers

General Information-
Stanford University
Stanford, CA 94305

Control:
Private

Academic Calendar:
Quarter

Religious Affiliation:
None

Founded:
1891

Web Site:
http://www.stanford.edu

Main Phone:
(650) 723-2300

Admissions Phone:
(650) 723-4291

Student Body

**Full-Time
Undergraduates:**
6,506

**Part-Time
Undergraduates:**
49

**Total Male
Undergraduates:**
3,430

**Total Female
Undergraduates:**
3,125

Admissions

Overall Acceptance Rate:
13%

Total Applicants:
19,172

Total Acceptances:
2,486

Freshman Enrollment:
1,648

Yield (% of admitted students who actually enroll):
70%

Early Decision Available?
No

Early Action Available?
Yes, Single Choice

Regular Decision Deadline:
December 15

Regular Decision Notification:
April 1

Must Reply-By Date:
May 1

Students Enrolled From Waiting List:
56

Transfer Applications Received:
1,345

Transfer Applications Accepted:
100

Transfer Students Enrolled:
78

Transfer Application Acceptance Rate:
7%

Common Application Accepted?
No

Supplemental Forms?
Yes

Admissions E-mail:
admission@stanford.edu

Admissions Web Site:
http://admission.stanford.edu

SAT I or ACT Required?
Yes, either is acceptable

First-Year Students Submitting SAT Scores:
98%

SAT I Range (25th – 75th Percentile):
1370 – 1550

SAT I Verbal Range (25th – 75th Percentile):
680 – 770

SAT I Math Range (25th – 75th Percentile):
690 – 780

SAT II Requirements:
3 subject tests highly recommended (though not required); one should be Writing and another should be Math 2C.

SAT II Requirements:
3 subject tests highly
recommended (though not
required); one should be
Writing and another should be
Math 2C.

**Top 10% of High
School Class:**
87%

Retention Rate:
98%

Application Fee:
$75

Financial Information

Full-Time Tuition:
$31,200

Room and Board:
$9,932

Books and Supplies for Class:
$1,260

**Average Need-Based
Financial Aid Package
(including loans, work-study,
grants, and other sources):**
$28,600

**Students Who
Applied For Financial Aid:**
54%

Students Who Received Aid:
84%

Financial Aid Forms Deadline:
February 1

Financial Aid Phone:
(650) 723-3058

Financial Aid E-mail:
financialaid@stanford.edu

Financial Aid Web Site:
http://www.stanford.edu/dept/
finaid

Academics

The Lowdown On...
Academics

Degrees Awarded:
Bachelor
Master
Doctorate

Undergraduate Schools:
Humanities and Sciences
Engineering
Earth Sciences

Most Popular Majors:
10% Economics
10% Interdisciplinary Studies
 8% Biology
 7% Computer Science
 6% Psychology

→

Full-Time Faculty:
949

Student-to-Faculty Ratio:
6:1

Faculty with Terminal Degree:
99%

Average Course Load:
15 quarter units

Special Degree Options
Co-terminal Master's degrees possible in most departments

Honors (thesis)

AP Test Score Requirements
Possible credit for scores of 4 or 5

IB Test Score Requirements
Possible credit for scores of 5, 6, or 7

Best Places to Study
Green Library Stacks, The CoHo (coffee house), Bender Room, Law Library

Sample Academic Clubs
Society of Black Scientists and Engineers, Society of Women Engineers, Stanford Debate Society, Stanford Economics Association; for more information see *http://osa.stanford. edu/studentgroups*

Did You Know?

Many of **Stanford's Computer Science and Electrical Engineering classes** are offered on television or through video, and are available on the Internet.

Stanford is on the quarter system. Students typically attend three quarters each year: autumn, winter, and spring. Courses are measured in units, where each unit roughly corresponds to three hours of work per week. It takes 180 units to graduate, and on average, students enroll in 15 units per quarter.

Every quarter during the week before finals (called **Dead Week**), students gather at midnight to partake in a tradition called the "Primal Scream."

Students Speak Out On...
Academics

{ **"The professors here are excellent. The personal attention you receive from your professors—all of whom are among the best in their field—is unbelievable."**

Q "Everyone seems to be **extraordinarily organized and on top of things**. Professors will bend over backwards to help you out."

Q "Some are the most distinguished in their field and are **wonderful lecturers**. Others could care less about undergraduates."

Q "Professors here are unlike any others I've ever seen. All those that I've had definitely expressed a genuine interest in their students. We have **world-renowned names** here, and most professors are at the top of their fields."

Q "Most of the professors here are pretty good. I mean, a lot have done amazing things, and they really know what they're talking about. **Of course, you get the occasional dud who's just old and boring** and such, but there are definitely quality teachers here. All the professors hold office hours, so if you make the effort, you can definitely get to know your professor. They're almost always available, too."

Q "To be honest, I didn't really feel like I had a good relationship with a professor until senior year. When you start out as a freshman, you have to take **a lot of large lecture classes with sections and TAs**. Those classes tend to feel a lot more competitive, and it's easier to get lost in the crowd if you're not the most vocal student."

Q "The information that my professors presented was fascinating. The **professors here at Stanford are some of the best in the world**, and not only are they the top minds in their fields, they also know how to teach in a way that is comprehensible to a beginner."

Q "They are generally nice and willing to help you if you need help; though, **depending on your major, they may be more interested in their research** than in your education. But the teaching assistants (TAs) are usually great. The IHUM program that all freshmen have to go through [Introduction to the Humanities] is lame and harsh, and you'll probably get your first B or B+ in this program during at least one quarter—most people do. But it can be pretty cool."

Q "Some are great, some are terrible, some are burnt out, and some have tons of prestige and insight. **My best teacher was a graduate student** who was just ridiculously excited about his field of study."

Q "In my experience, professors really want students to come to their office. They like talking to the undergraduates. **Most dorms have 'faculty nights,'** where everyone can invite professors to come have a nicer-than-usual dinner."

Q "The computer science classes are top-notch, but be prepared to spend oodles of time cooped up in your room programming. **Teachers are quite accessible**, but you'll find you won't have time to talk to them because of said programming."

Q "You couldn't ask for anything better. It's quite an experience to take an economics class from someone who helped rebuild Russia's economy after the collapse of Communism, or physics from Nobel prize winners. And the **teachers will generally take more time out of their days to talk to undergrads than students need**! Most of my classes have been interesting and even exiting."

Q "Most of my professors take the time to create a course outline, prepare for their lectures, and have office hours to answer student questions. **Competition is stiff**, and there is rarely enough time to fully study and understand the material taught in the classes."

Q "For the most part, the professors at Stanford are wonderful, accomplished people who are active in their field and are dedicated to teaching undergrads. Of course, there are always exceptions, but **I have yet to encounter a truly horrendous teacher at Stanford**. Even professors who you may not get along with are probably brilliant researchers, so every faculty member has something to offer."

Q "My best experiences with classes at Stanford by far have been the small classes that I took my junior and senior years. And even among those, my most rewarding classes were taught by certain professors who make it clear to the class that **they care about undergrads**."

Q "The majority of professors are bright, articulate, and have contributed enormously to their field. It's more the student's responsibility to **overcome the fear** of confronting someone like that in a small office. But once you've gotten over the 'office-hour hump,' you'll find that most teachers enjoy speaking one-on-one with students, and are not so intimidating after all."

The College Prowler Take On...
Academics

Most Stanford students are quite pleased with their academic experiences. Classes are interesting and intellectually stimulating. Professors are highly accessible, and truly make an effort to get to know undergraduates. Some students may feel that their introductory classes are too large, or poorly designed, but the overwhelming sentiment is that the education you get here truly is first-rate. It seems Stanford and its faculty are doing everything possible to make the academic experience top-notch.

Some of the problems with Stanford's academics have more to do with the students than the faculty. There are a lot of passionless pre-professionals at Stanford. There are the pre-meds who are still in high-school mode—packing in extracurriculars, and above all else maintaining high GPAs and studying for the MCATs. Many economic majors openly admit that they don't even like their major, but hope to end up in investment-banking. In engineering, half of the students don't even appear to like the classes—which are completely time-consuming and exhausting—but they put up with it because it's their ticket to success. The most driven students in the country end up here, and they get what they want, eventually. However, there are many students who are passionate about their studies. But let's face it, for the price you have to pay to go here, you are expecting a big payoff in the end. For many, the simple prospect of becoming an enlightened, educated individual just isn't enough.

A+

The College Prowler® Grade on
Academics: A+

A high Academics grade generally indicates that professors are knowledgeable, accessible, and genuinely interested in their students' welfare. Other determining factors include class size, how well professors communicate, and whether or not classes are engaging.

Local Atmosphere

The Lowdown On...
Local Atmosphere

Region:
Palo Alto/Silicon Valley

City, State:
Stanford, CA

Setting:
Suburban

Distance from San Francisco:
1 hour

Distance from San Jose:
30 minutes

Distance from Los Angeles:
6 hours

Points of Interest:
Dot-Coms
Foothills
Half Moon Bay
San Francisco
Santa Cruz

→

Closest Movie Theatres:

Aquarius Movie Theater
430 Emerson Street
Palo Alto, CA 94031
(650) 266-9260

CineArts at Palo Alto
3000 El Camino Real at
Page Mill Road
Palo Alto, CA 94306
(650) 493-3456

Century 16 Mountain View
1500 North Shoreline
Boulevard, Mountain View,
CA 94043
(650) 960-0970

Major Sports Teams:

49ers (football)

Giants (baseball)

Warriors (basketball)

Closest Shopping Malls:

San Antonio Shopping Center
Stanford Shopping Center

City Web Sites

http://www.city.palo-alto.ca.us
http://www.ci.sf.ca.us

Did You Know?

5 Fun Facts about Stanford:

- Stanford's campus is a whopping **8,180 acres**, only a third of which is heavily developed.

- Prior to becoming a university, Stanford's land was **a stock farm used for breeding horses**; hence Stanford's nickname, "The Farm."

- In addition to **25,000 trees, a lake, and 670 buildings**, Stanford's campus is also home to its very own 49-megawatt power plant.

- Stanford contains a winding network of **underground steam tunnels**. Most of the openings have been sealed off, but it is a popular undergrad pastime to find the few unsealed manholes and explore the system illegally at night.

- Stanford's land contains **SLAC**, a two mile, linear accelerator operated by Stanford for the U.S. Department of Energy.

Local Slang:

Hella – "very" or "really," as in "These pants are hella tight."

Frisco – a shortened word for San Francisco; locals neither say, nor approve of this phrase

Dank – Marijuana

Famous People from the Bay Area:

Ken Kesey, Jerry Yang, Allen Ginsberg, Steve Jobs, Robert Frost, Jerry Garcia, William Randolph Hearst, Sidney Howard, Jack London, George Lucas, John Steinbeck, Teri Hatcher, Alicia Silverstone

"There are some great restaurants off campus, but most of them are quite pricey. There are a few bars, but I haven't found a single good dance spot. I go to 'Frisco' to party."

Q "It's Palo Alto. It's a pretty regular town, but **it is close to San Francisco**, which has a lot of good stuff to do."

Q "Palo Alto is a small, upscale town. Mountain View, to the south, is more of a 'normal' town area, and Atherton, to the north, is one of the most exclusive, blue-blood places in the nation. **There's not much to see off campus until you get to San Jose and Silicon Valley**, which are about 20 minutes to the south, or 'the city,' which is about 40 minutes to the north. Be forewarned that rush hour travel is terrible here, but that affects very few students because the majority lives on campus."

Q "Palo Alto is a wealthy community with little to do except watch movies and eat. San Francisco has all of the excitement. **I go to a jazz club in Oakland a lot**."

Q "In the town of Palo Alto, there's not much to do. But there is the Great America theme park a little bit south of here, San Francisco to the north, and **lots of movie theatres and such around town**."

Q "**Palo Alto is the worst college town ever**. It's mostly boring, and anything you might do here is usually expensive. There are no schools in the immediate area, although there are a few schools in San Jose and San Francisco. There's not much stuff either to stay away from or visit. San Francisco is really fun though; if you come here, you should go there a lot. Berkeley provides a much better college-town atmosphere, as well."

Q "Palo Alto is mostly a place where Silicon Valley computer guys live. It's kind of far from campus, therefore, it isn't much of a student hangout. **It's a nice place to go if you want to go out to dinner every once in a while**."

Q "Palo Alto is definitely not a college town! There is a dire shortage of 24-hour places, although more stores are gradually extending their hours. **There is a plethora of good restaurants on University Avenue**, but they are by no means cheap. Shopping at Stanford Shopping Center is pricey, too. In other words, Palo Alto is an affluent town, and the shops cater to residents, not to college students. You'll have to go to Berkeley to get a college-town feel."

Q "We live close to Palo Alto, **a relatively affluent town boasting clean streets and elegant restaurants**. Most students complain that Palo Alto is too boring, though, and that there is nothing to do. While Palo Alto may not have the liveliness of a more traditional college town, it has its unique charms. I must concede that Palo Alto is not cheap. Meals cost about $10-$15, but most people do not mind so much because they eat in the dorms most of the time and come to Palo Alto only once or twice a week, due to the demanding nature of their studies. You may not find raging parties or cheap, hole-in-the-wall restaurants in Palo Alto, but you will find a safe and elegant setting to go to for a quick break from your studies."

Q "All I can say is that you need a car around here. Palo Alto is expensive, so if you don't mind blowing $15 a night on dinner when everyone wants to go out, then you'll be fine. Otherwise, **you have to drive a bit to find most movie theaters**, cheaper food, the beach, nightlife, and other amenities. After a year at Stanford, you'll think the city of Berkeley is college heaven."

Q "Palo Alto is a great place to be, and **it's only 45 minutes away from San Francisco**, so that's cool."

Q "**We live in a kind of bubble here at Stanford**, which is both a positive and a negative thing."

The College Prowler Take On...
Local Atmosphere

Student feelings about Palo Alto range from neutral to unsatisfied. It's a yuppie town with restaurants and activities to match. Students are happy with the food offerings and the safety of Palo Alto but don't think of it as a college town. Campus is large and isolated, so you either need access to a car or the patience to endure public transportation in order to explore. Still, if you manage to get out of the bubble, the Bay Area has a lot to offer. There's San Francisco, Berkeley, and San Jose, as well as many beautiful nature preserves. People also venture to Tahoe or Yosemite National Park.

As freshmen, most students are happy with the local atmosphere. Going into Palo Alto is a special treat reserved for a couple times a month. You'll be happy eating most of your meals in the dining hall and finding your fun at campus events. Plus, the standard freshman experience involves trips to San Francisco, Tahoe, Yosemite, Half Moon Bay, and other areas. Despite the natural beauty and pristine cities of the Bay Area, many agree that the region is currently experiencing a downturn. Any time of day, you will notice huge amounts of traffic. The region is so nice that everyone wants to be here. There were plans to make BART (the region's subway system) come all the way down and around the Bay. This would do wonders to help the traffic problems, but in Silicon Valley, and especially around Palo Alto, local pressure has prevented these developments.

B-

The College Prowler® Grade on

Local
Atmosphere: B-

A high Local Atmosphere grade indicates that the area surrounding campus is safe and scenic. Other factors include nearby attractions, proximity to other schools, and the town's attitude toward students.

Safety & Security

The Lowdown On...
Safety & Security

Number of Stanford University Police:
22 sworn officers,
22 community service officers

Phone:
(650) 723-9633

Safety Services:
5-SURE escort service,
Emergency phones, CSARRT
(Campus Sexual Assault Rape
Recovery Team)

Health Services:
Vaden Health Center (SHPRC)

Free STD Screening – including
HIV/AIDS testing

Free women's health exams

The Bridge – the peer
counseling center

On-site pharmeceuticals

Stanford Hospital

PHEs – Peer Health
Educators who live as
staff in large dormitories

Health Center Office Hours:
Monday-Friday 8 a.m.-8 p.m.;
Saturday and Sunday
10 a.m.-5:30 p.m.

Students Speak Out On...
Safety & Security

"Security is really good. They have blue phones, which are conveniently located for you to use if you ever feel unsafe. Just don't leave your bike unlocked, because it will get stolen."

Q "Campus security is **outstanding**."

Q "Security and safety are awesome. **I can leave my things anywhere and not worry about them** getting stolen. My female friends never worry about walking around on campus at night, although I would still suggest that you walk with someone. There are campus emergency phones everywhere that you can use if you are in trouble. I would give security a 10 out of 10."

Q "It's extremely safe. **There are a few thefts in the dorms every year**, but Stanford is basically a self-contained community, so it's not a big issue."

Q "I feel very safe on campus. **Campus is like a happy little bubble**. Recently, there was a report of an assault on campus, but I have never experienced anything like that personally. Generally, the biggest thing we have to worry about is high school kids skateboarding around campus and trying to sneak into our frat parties."

Q "It's really safe here; I've never felt that I was ever in danger of anything. **I often walk or bike around campus** alone at night and feel fine about it. Of course, I wouldn't recommend walking alone in totally isolated places on campus, but that's true of anyplace, not just Stanford."

Q "There are a lot of lights and stuff all over campus, and there are always students around. In terms of other safety issues, I have had bikes stolen, just like a lot of students here have. But I think that problem can be solved quite easily by **investing in a good U-lock** for your bike instead of a cheap cable lock like I had. Those can be cut quite easily. In terms of other safety issues, Stanford feels very safe."

Q "Stanford is very safe. People run around campus at all hours of the night. **There are plenty of well-lit streets**, and the campus is relatively private."

Q "Stanford is one of the safest campuses that I've ever visited. Everything is out in the open, and we all look out for one another, even though that's not usually necessary. Stanford is like a bubble— **everything that happens within Stanford is totally contained** because it is sealed off from the world."

Q "I would say that Stanford is a relatively safe campus, but the few visible safety mechanisms available are not really up-to-snuff. For example, many of the blue emergency telephones scattered on campus are out of order, which can be kind of scary on a campus this large. **All in all, though, I feel really safe at Stanford**."

Q "Campus is perfectly safe. **I have been out running numerous times past midnight**, and I never felt any concern for my safety."

Q "I have felt so safe at Stanford. Granted, I don't walk around all the time at night in dark areas by myself, because I'll either bike or be with other people. **I've never had anything stolen**, and I never had anything bad happen to me or to a friend. Some people will leave all their books and their laptop at the library for hours while they go eat, and no one takes their stuff."

Q "**Bike theft is the biggest issue**, but the key is to ride a really old one that no one wants, and then you won't have to deal with that. I've also heard of people getting their laptops stolen out of their dorm rooms, but that's pretty much the extent of it."

The College Prowler Take On...
Safety & Security

Students are overwhelmingly satisfied with the level of campus safety. Given the huge size and isolated nature of campus, it is rare that outsiders venture here at night. The police forces are adequate, and they do a good job of patrolling. It is so safe that students feel at ease when walking or biking around late at night. Students may even leave their dorm rooms unlocked without any problems. The only crime that occurs frequently is bike theft. Sometimes—especially during move-in and move-out periods—there can be more serious theft from dorms, including laptops and other expensive electronics, but this is easily avoided by locking your door.

Though often viewed as a bad thing, the Stanford "bubble" phenomenon does create a very safe and secure environment. If you're at a campus party, you can safely stumble back home. If you're 21, you don't even have to worry about carrying alcohol, as the current University policy does not have an open-container rule. It is true that a large number of the blue safety lights have been out of order for a while, but these are rarely used. Chances are, you will have a cell-phone anyway. The only noteworthy crimes that have occurred on campus recently are a series of "bike-by" groping incidents. Aside from this, Stanford has very few problems of this nature. So just keep your bike and laptop securely locked, and you probably won't be the victim of any serious crime at Stanford.

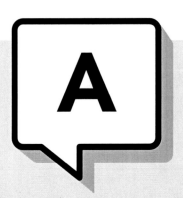

The College Prowler® Grade on

Safety & Security: A

A high grade in Safety & Security means that students generally feel safe, campus police are visible, blue-light phones and escort services are readily available, and safety precautions are not overly necessary.

Computers

The Lowdown On...
Computers

High-Speed Network?
Two T1 lines dedicated to
student residential use

Wireless Network?
Yes, throughout the Main
Quad, Green and Meyer
Libraries, Stern, and
Wilbur Hall

Number of Labs:
5

Number of Computers:
1,000

Operating Systems:
Mac OS X, Windows 2000,
RedHat Linux, Solaris Unix

24-Hour Labs:
Meyer, Sweet Hall, Tresidder,
dorm clusters

Software on Computer Clusters

Adobe Acrobat Professional 6.0, Adobe Illustrator 10, Adobe Indesign 2, Adobe Photoshop 7.0, Audacity 1.0.0, Codewarrior Pro 8.0, Extend 6.0, Eviews 4.1, Final Cut Pro 4, Fugu, KeyServer 6, MacOSX Developer Tools, Macromedia Dreamweaver MX 6.0, Macromedia Fireworks MX 6.0, Macromedia Flash MX 6.0, Mathematica 6, MATLAB 5.2.1, Microsoft Office, Microsoft Visual Studio .NET, Roxio Easy CD Creator, and SPSS 11

Discounted Software

All software, including Mac and Windows operating systems, MS Office, Macromedia, and others, are typically offered at a 30 to 50 percent discount.

Free Software

Eudora, Symantec AntiVirus

Charge to Print?

$0.10 per page

Did You Know?

SUN Microsystems, which was started by Stanford graduate students, originally stood for Stanford University Network.

Students Speak Out On...
Computers

"Students get a fast connection from their dorm room if they have a computer. Every dorm has a computer cluster with a lot of computers in it. The clusters are usually not too crowded."

Q "The labs are usually not busy, but around finals they are at their worst; while midterm weeks vary depending on the class, finals are on the same days for everyone. **If you can afford it, get your own computer**. My roommate is a pre-med and psychology double major and hasn't bought one for the last three years, but I think that it's worth it to be able to hook up to the network."

Q "Dorm computer clusters usually only get crowded around midterms and finals. There are **24-hour computer clusters in the middle of campus** that are almost never full. Bringing your own computer will prove to be very convenient, though."

Q "It's always good to have your own computer, but every residence hall has its own computer cluster with three or four computers in it. **They all have super fast internet connections** and are not usually crowded."

Q "Campus clusters are **90 percent Macintosh**."

Q "The computer labs are almost never crowded. Most people bring their own computers. Actually, **I don't know anybody who doesn't have their own computer**, so I would say bring one."

Q "There are tons of computer labs and great computer support on this campus. **There is an RCC (Residential Computer Consultant) that lives in every dorm or house**. He or she is usually like an extra RA (resident assistant) who can also fix your computer. My only complaint would be that sometimes our download times are slower than they should be. I heard Stanford used to have a T3 line but decided to get rid of it and go back to multiple, slower T1 lines, mainly because students were hogging bandwidth for media exchanges. On a side note, Stanford seems to be totally in favor of such media exchange programs."

Q "This is Silicon Valley, so there is **never a shortage of computers**."

Q "**The computer network is awesome**, as expected. Computer labs are usually crowded only the few nights before big CS projects are due. Bringing your own computer is recommended, if only for the file-sharing opportunities."

Q "The computer network is easy to use, unless you get nailed by a virus. Computer labs are fine, but no one really uses them. **Definitely bring a computer freshman year**—DJ Winamp has proved to be a must-have!"

Q "I have had a computer all four years, but actually wrote most essays on cluster computers for two of those years. **The computers are all actually really nice and new**, but I definitely experienced my share of computer traumas during my time here—from crashes, to printer issues, to losing pages of papers."

Q "**Most students have computers here**, so it's hard to imagine getting by without one, but it can be done. It's cheaper, and it'll teach you to love Pine [e-mail service]."

Q "The computer network is excellent. It's very fast, and despite occasional hacker attacks, tends to be quite reliable. **Wireless Internet access is becoming increasingly widespread**, which is a wonderful trend for those of us with laptops. Every dorm has a computer cluster with, at minimum, several Macs, a PC, and a laser printer. The clusters get a pretty good amount of use, but they usually aren't crowded."

Q "I highly recommend bringing your own computer. **Every room has high-speed Internet access**, and it's remarkably convenient to be able to check your e-mail, Web browse, and IM from your own room. It's much better to have a laptop than a desktop machine. Laptops allow you to take your computer with you when you study away from your room, and with the spread of wireless internet access, you can go online from a lot of places. Most importantly, you don't need to worry about storing a laptop over the summer."

The College Prowler Take On...
Computers

Students are very happy with the quality and quantity of computing resources at Stanford. The network is reasonably fast, and there are many well-maintained labs. Students generally recommend bringing your own computer; in particular, a laptop. However, if you don't bring one, you'll still be okay. The campus is heavily wired, and there are plenty of technical people around to help if you have problems. Every dorm and house includes a staff member called the Residential Computer Consultant, who is hired to help residents keep their computers running.

Stanford's Internet services might actually be considered a bit slow, given the Silicon Valley location and heavy emphasis on computing. There are occasional outages, and sometimes bandwidth is a bit scarce for connecting to the outside world. For most regular users, however, the network will be more than sufficient. It should be noted that the local area network is excellent. Most residents in the dorms are using iTunes these days, so there's always interesting music floating around. In addition, the computer labs are state-of-the-art. There is definitely an emphasis on Mac over PC, but PCs can still be found. It is also great to have a computer cluster right in your own dorm, which you can use anytime your roommate is making too much noise, your own computer is having a problem, or if you don't have your own printer. Also, Stanford's Unix lab is truly top-notch. For engineering classes, you will most likely work from Sweet Hall directly on the various Unix/Linux boxes, or you can connect remotely from your own computer to use them.

The College Prowler® Grade on
Computers: A

A high grade in Computers designates that computer labs are available, the computer network is easily accessible, and the campus' computing technology is up-to-date.

Facilities

The Lowdown On...
Facilities

Student Center:
Tresidder Union

Athletic Center:
Tresidder Fitness, Arrillaga
Fitness Center, Roble Gym

Libraries:
25

Campus Size:
8,180 acres

Popular Places to Chill:
The CoHo, dorm lounges,
The Oval, The Treehouse,
Tresidder Union

→

What Is There to Do?

You can work out, go swimming, grab a DVD from the library, get a sandwich or some Mexican food at Tresidder, or just lie around in the sun.

Movie Theatre on Campus?

No

Bowling on Campus?

No

Bar on Campus?

Both The Treehouse and The CoHo serve beer.

Favorite Things to Do?

Flicks [student movie service] is a popular diversion on a Sunday evening when you should be doing your homework. A couple thousand people cram into Memorial Auditorium and have a rowdy paper fight before the show. If that's not your scene, you can check out just about any DVD that exists from Green Library for free. Watch it in your dorm, or on one of the many publicly available projection screens on campus.

Students Speak Out On...
Facilities

"The facilities here are awesome. The gyms are nice, and so are the computer labs. It's a private school, so there is nice stuff pretty much everywhere."

Q "As far as athletic facilities are concerned, we have a couple of small gyms. **I hear that the Arrillaga Gym is pretty good**, but I've never been there, and most of the time, its use is restricted to our athletes. The student center flat-out sucks, especially compared to Berkeley or UCLA."

Q "There are two major places to work out here. One has more limited hours, because the athletes work out there a lot. The other, called the Tresidder Fitness Center, has fewer machines. People love to complain about Tresidder, but it's really not that bad. **Our student union leaves a lot to be desired**. There aren't many places to eat, and it just doesn't seem like a place in which you would want to hang out very much. The computer facilities are great. I have my own computer, but sometimes I go to a lab just to get away from the distractions of dorm life. I have always been able to find a computer when I needed one."

Q "Our athletic and computer facilities are the best out of any university that I've ever seen. **The student union needs some work**, though."

Q "The only **thing that we don't have on campus is a real student union** where everybody can hang out."

Q "Every summer they build something new. Most people say this is **one of the nation's prettiest campuses**."

Q "Campus is in the midst of renovation, so some stuff might be inaccessible, but most of the facilities are relatively new. Some of the **newly-finished classrooms have neat gadgets**."

Q "You'd think with all of Stanford's money we'd have better stuff. The **athletes have the best athletic facilities in the country**, but if you're a normal student and want to use the gym, the facilities are definitely lacking. Also, there's really no student center."

Q "**Facilities at Stanford range from excellent to atrocious**. On the atrocious side of things falls Tresidder Fitness—the most conveniently located gym here. It's in the student union, and it's a really unpleasant place to work out—small with old machines that are not cleaned or repaired with any decent frequency. It's almost always crowded, so you have to wait in lines to use certain machines. Also on the atrocious side is Tresidder itself. If you are over 21 then you can have fun drinking at The Treehouse or The Coho, but otherwise there isn't much to eat, and there certainly isn't much to do. Certain places here, however, are very nice and quite fancy."

Q "The **facilities on campus are generally newer** and very well maintained. All that tuition money has to go somewhere, doesn't it? The 'student union' is something of a disappointment. The available food there isn't the greatest, and amenities like an arcade or a bowling alley are completely absent."

The College Prowler Take On...
Facilities

Student opinions on facilities at Stanford are fairly consistent. Students are pleased with computer clusters, labs, and libraries. These all provide a good venue for studying and getting work done. However, students are unified in their distaste for the current student union, Tresidder. The food options in the union aren't particularly enticing, and there's little to do beyond sitting around at the coffeehouse. The student community doesn't focus around the union in any way, and many feel that there simply *isn't* a student center under current conditions. Opinions are somewhat mixed on athletic facilities. Most think there are some reasonable options for working out on campus. Some, however, think that these facilities are overly crowded, or don't have convenient hours.

Well, it's now out in the open that Stanford students are dissatisfied with Tresidder Union, and the University is trying to do something about it. The bottom floor of the union has been revamped, and a Subway and coffeehouse were added.

B

The College Prowler® Grade on

Facilities: B

A high Facilities grade indicates that the campus is aesthetically pleasing and well-maintained; facilities are state-of-the-art, and libraries are exceptional. Other determining factors include the quality of both athletic and student centers and an abundance of things to do on campus.

Campus Dining

The Lowdown On...
Campus Dining

Freshman Meal Plan Requirement?

Yes, all freshmen are required to live on campus and get a meal plan.

Meal Plan Average Cost:

$4,656 per year

Places to Grab a Bite with Your Meal Plan:

The basic meal plan for freshmen is usable at any of the main eating halls.

Branner

Food: American
Location: Branner Dormitory
Favorite Dish: Upper Crust Pizza
Hours: Lunch, 11:45 a.m.-12:45 p.m.; Dinner, 5:30 p.m.-6:30 p.m.; closed weekends

Florence Moore

Food: Italian and American
Location: Florence
Moore Dormitory
Favorite Dish: shwarma kabobs
Hours: Monday-Thursday,
Breakfast, 8 a.m.-10 a.m.;
Lunch, 11:30 a.m.-1 p.m.;
Dinner, 5 p.m.-8 p.m.;
Sunday brunch, 10:30 a.m.-
12:30 p.m.; Dinner, 5 p.m.-
6:45 p.m.

Lakeside

Food: variety, late-night snacks
Location: Lagunita Dormitory
Favorite Dish: fresh pizza
Hours: Monday-Friday,
Breakfast, 7:30 a.m.-9:30
a.m.; Lunch, 11:30 a.m.-1:15
p.m.; Dinner, 5:15 p.m.-8 p.m.
Weekends, Brunch, 10 a.m.-
1 p.m.; Dinner, 5 p.m.-7 p.m.;
Late Night, Sunday-Thursday,
9:30 p.m.-2 a.m.

Manzanita

Food: variety, late-night snacks
Location: Kimball Dormitory
Favorite Dish: anything from
the grille
Hours: Monday-Friday, Lunch,
11:30 a.m.-1:15 p.m.; Dinner,
5 p.m.-6:45 p.m.

The Marketplace at Wilbur

Food: variety, snacks
Location: WIlbur Hall
Favorite Dish: omelets
and quesadillas
Hours: Monday-Friday,
Breakfast 7:30 a.m.-9:30 a.m.;
Lunch, 11:30 a.m.-1:15 p.m.;
Dinner, 5:15 p.m.-7:15 p.m.;
Weekends, Brunch: 10:30 a.m.-
12:30 p.m.; Dinner:
5:15-7:15pm

Ricker Dining

Food: grill, pizzas
Location: Governer's Corner
Favorite Dish: organic fruits
and vegetables
Hours: Monday-Thursday,
Continental Breakfast,
7:30 a.m.-9:30 a.m.; Lunch,
11:45 a.m.-1 p.m.; Dinner,
5:15 p.m.-6:45 p.m.; Sunday
Brunch, 10:30 a.m.-12:30 p.m.;
Dinner, 5:15 a.m.-6:45 p.m.

Stern Dining and Cyber Cafe

Food: Latin
Location: Casa Zapata
Hours: Monday-Friday,
Continental Breakfast, 8 a.m.-
10 a.m.; Lunch, 11:30 a.m.-
1:15 p.m.; Dinner, 5:15 p.m.-
8 p.m.; Weekends, Brunch,
10 a.m.-1 p.m.; Dinner:
5 p.m.-7:15 p.m.

Thai Cafe

Food: Thai
Location: Jordan Hall
Favorite Dish: Peanut
sauce salad
Hours: Monday-Friday 11:30
a.m.-1:40 p.m.

The Treehouse

Food: Mexican, grill
Location: Tresidder
Favorite Dish: Steak Ranchero
Hours: Monday-Friday 10 a.m.-
1 a.m., Saturday-Sunday
10 a.m.-12 a.m.

Off-Campus Places to Use Your Meal Plan

None

24-Hour On-Campus Eating?

There is no such thing at Stanford. However, if you live in a row
house, you will have an open kitchen. You can grab a snack here,
or find some leftovers any hour of the day.

Other Options

Tresidder offers several food options. These include: Subway, The
Treehouse (Mexican), Jamba Juice (smoothies), The Coho (pizza,
sandwiches, and beverages), Pete's Coffee, and Tresidder Express
(convenience store with sandwiches, chips, and candy).

The Truck

During lunch hours, a truck parks behind the student union.
For $5 you can fill a container with as much pan-Asian food as
possible. It's enough food to split with someone.

Students Speak Out On...
Campus Dining

{ **"The food on campus isn't very good. However, when you come to campus for freshman orientation, they give you a listing of all the off-campus eating places, and almost all of them are good."**

Q "**There's good food at the dorms**. The smaller houses have better food and fully stocked public kitchens. Restaurants in Palo Alto are fairly good, but some are expensive."

Q "Manzanita Park has good food. The Tresidder Memorial Union has Jamba Juice, and the coffeehouse, the CoHo, is also there. Dorm food isn't great, and some kinds are better than others. **Try a meal plan with points** because it allows you more flexibility in eating. Also, you can eat in any dining dorm on campus, so just ask around and find a good place."

Q "The **Tresidder Union is probably your best bet** for restaurant-style dining."

Q "Dorm food is pretty good, but it depends on where you live. Some dorms have better food than others, but **none of the food is so bad that it will kill you**. There is a Mexican restaurant and a coffeehouse on campus that are alternatives to the dorm food. I don't complain about the food, although I do try to go off campus for a meal once a week, just for a change from dorm food."

Q "Dorm food at Stanford is better than the food at most schools, from what I've heard. As far as on-campus restaurants go, the only two places that I'd really recommend are **the Treehouse and the Jordan Hall Thai Cafe**, which is only open around lunch."

Q "The dining halls here are above-average, but their fare gets repetitive after a while. **There are a lot of good little places on campus**, but no chain restaurants."

Q "I'm not a picky eater, so I think that all the food is okay. I definitely like some places more than others, but since most of **the dining halls have been revamped** within the last few years, they're all pretty good."

Q "There are some random places that you can go to, like Jamba Juice and other small shops in the Tresidder Union. **You don't have to worry about being unable to find quality food**."

Q "The food here is definitely better than the food on any other campus. **The food here was actually ranked nationally** in terms of quality compared to other campuses. Pretty much any of the dorms, especially Wilbur and Manzanita, have good food."

Q "On-campus food is terrible. Dining services have this monopoly where they control every option for eating on campus, and the result is pretty bad. The **best options are definitely eating clubs**, but drawing into a place that offers eating clubs is pretty difficult."

Q "**On-campus food is not that bad**, but I suppose it's all relative. Be sure to praise Miss Florence Moore, who donated enough money to the school to have a dorm and cafeteria built in her name, and she demanded that ice cream be served at every meal."

Q "The food on campus **ranges from not quite abysmal to pretty dang good**, but it all depends on where you live. If you're stuck in a dorm with a bad dining hall (FloMo), you have few options, because a good dining hall (Wilbur) may be on a different meal plan system that is not compatible with yours. It kind of sucks. Also, Stanford has few on-campus, non-dining-hall eateries, so there aren't a whole lot of options for food."

Q "Dining hall food is pretty decent. If you're in university housing (which most folk are for all four years), you are required to purchase your dorm's type of meal plan. This can mean paying a lot for not much food if you're someone who likes to eat at odd hours or misses meal times. But if you are a big eater who doesn't eat out too often, you can do quite well. **I'd recommend against Wilbur Hall's dining if at all possible**, as it's on an á la carte system. At the prices they charge, big eaters fare pretty badly. The food is good, however, as the hall was recently renovated, and people with smaller appetites tend to enjoy it."

Q "The **co-ops and self-ops at Stanford are two of the most unique things** about the dining system. Students either do the cooking themselves or hire a chef. This means less variety on a given night, but the food is usually very good and much cheaper, too."

The College Prowler Take On...
Campus Dining

Stanford's on-campus dining should be given credit for what it manages to do right. In the case of the dormitory cafeterias, food is generally high quality. The fruits and vegetables are appropriately Californian and excellent. Lunches are usually interesting, with both healthy and unhealthy options. Dinners tend to be less exciting, but still hearty and nutritious. Anyone can get tired of the dining hall after several months of it, but there are ways to keep it interesting. Try some different sandwiches at lunch, and avoid the dining halls on Saturday nights when they serve the tired Italian meatloaf, and go out with some friends instead.

The biggest problem that students have with Stanford dining is that participation is mandatory. If you live in a dorm, you have to get the meal plan. If you have a medical or religious reason for not being able to participate, you must go to great lengths to prove it, then you must pay around $350 per quarter to opt out of the meal plan. If you have a strange schedule and miss a lot of meals, Stanford Dining will try to help you, but they still make you participate. If you choose to get the smallest meal plan available, you will only save five to eight percent off the price of the largest meal plan. Most students snicker whenever the colorful posters around campus remind them of Stanford dining's slogan: "It's all about you."

The College Prowler® Grade on

Campus Dining: B

Our grade on Campus Dining addresses the quality of both school-owned dining halls and independent on-campus restaurants as well as the price, availability, and variety of food.

Off-Campus Dining

The Lowdown On...
Off-Campus Dining

Restaurant Prowler:
Popular Places to Eat!

Applewood Pizza
Food: pizza
1001 El Camino Real, Menlo Park
(650) 324-3486
Cool Features: unusual toppings, beer on tap
Price: $8 and under per person
Hours: Monday-Friday 11 a.m.-2 p.m., and 5 p.m.-10 p.m.; Saturday 5 p.m-10 p.m.; Sunday 11 a.m.-2 p.m., and 5 p.m.-9 p.m.

Bella Luna
Food: Italian
233 University Ave.
(650) 329-0665
Cool Features: massive portions, family style dining
Price: $20 and under per person
Hours: Monday-Thursday 5 p.m.-10 p.m.; Friday 5 p.m.-11 p.m.; Saturday 12 p.m.-11 p.m.; Sunday 12 p.m.-10 p.m.

→

Buca di Beppo's

Food: Italian

643 Emerson Street

(650) 329-0665

Cool Features: massive portions, family style dining

Price: $20 and under per person

Hours: Monday-Thursday 5 p.m.-10 p.m.; Friday 5 p.m.-11 p.m.; Saturday 12 p.m.-11 p.m.; Sunday 12 p.m.-10 p.m.

California Pizza Kitchen

Food: gourmet pizza

531 Cowper Street

(650) 323-7332

Price: $15 and under per person

Hours: Monday-Sunday 11 a.m.-10 p.m.

Cold Stone Creamery

Food: ice cream

9 Town & Country Village

(650) 323-2102

Cool Features: cold-slab

Price: $5 and under per person

Hours: Monday-Friday 11 a.m.-3 p.m., 5 p.m.-10 p.m.; Saturday-Sunday 12 p.m.-10 p.m.

Darbar

Food: Indian / Pakistani

129 Lytton Avenue

(650) 321-6688

Cool Features: $7 lunch buffet

Price: $10 and under per person

Hours: Monday-Wednesday 11 a.m.-2:30 p.m., and 5 p.m.-9:30 p.m.; Thursday-Friday 11 a.m.-2:30 p.m., and 5 p.m.-10 p.m.; Saturday 5 p.m.-10 p.m.; Sunday 5 p.m.-9:30 p.m.

Denny's

Food: diner fare

4256 El Camino Real

(650) 493-3082

Cool Features: all-day breakfast

Price: $10 and under per person

Hours: Daily, 24 hours

The Fish Market

Food: seafood

3150 El Camino Real

(650) 493-9188

Cool Features: amazing sourdough bread, fresh fish

Price: $15 and under per person

Hours: Monday-Saturday Lunch 11 a.m.-5 p.m.. Sunday Lunch 12 p.m.-5 p.m.; Sunday-Thursday Dinner 5 p.m.-9:30 p.m.; Friday-Saturday Dinner 5 p.m.-10 p.m.

Frankie, Johnny, & Luigi Too!

Food: Italian

939 W. El Camino Real, Mountain View

(650) 967-5384

Cool Features: coupons and student discounts

Price: $10 and under per person

Hours: Monday-Thursday 11 a.m.-12 a.m.; Friday 11 a.m.-1 a.m.; Saturday 11:30 a.m.-1 a.m.; Sunday 11:30 a.m.-11 p.m.

Fresh Taste Mandarin Kitchen

Food: Chinese

2111 El Camino Real

(650) 324-8749

Cool Features: Student special

Price: $7 and under per person

Hours: Monday-Saturday 11:30 a.m.-2:30 p.m., and 5 p.m.-9:30 p.m.

Gelato Classico

Food: Italian ice cream

435 Emerson Street

(650) 327-1317

Cool Features: Unique flavors, like pumpkin and pear

Price: $3 and under per person

Hours: Sunday-Thursday 11:30 a.m.–10:30 p.m.; Friday-Saturday 11:30 a.m.-11 p.m.

Hobee's

Food: California breakfast

67 Town & Country Village

(650) 327-4111

Cool Features: coffeecake

Price: $7 and under per person

Hours: Monday-Friday 7 a.m.-9 p.m.; Saturday-Sunday 8 a.m.-9 p.m.

Hunan Garden

Food: Chinese

3345 El Camino Real

(650) 565-8868

Cool Features: good spicy options

Price: $10 and under per person

Hours: Monday-Sunday 11 a.m.-2:30 p.m., and 4:30 p.m.-9:30 p.m.

In-N-Out Burger

Food: premium burgers

1159 N. Rengstorff Avenue, Mountain View

1-800-786-1000

Cool Features: Try a Double-Double Animal Style, and get your fries crispy.

Price: $5 and under per person

Hours: Sunday-Thursday 10:30 a.m.-1 a.m.; Friday-Saturday 10:30 a.m.-1:30 a.m.

→

Janta Indian Cuisine

Food: Indian

369 Lytton Avenue

(650) 462-5903

Cool Features: many special meals for two

Price: $15 and under per person

Hours: Monday-Friday 11:30 a.m.-2:30 p.m., 5 p.m.-10 p.m.; Saturday Brunch, 12 p.m.-2:30 p.m., Dinner 5 p.m.-10 p.m.; Sunday 5 p.m.-10 p.m.

Jack-In-The-Box

Food: fast food

423 University Avenue

(650) 586-0350

Cool Features: 24-hour eating

Price: $7 and under per person

Hours: Daily, 24 hours

Krung Siam Thai Cuisine

Food: Thai

423 University Avenue

(650) 322-5900

Cool Features: pineapple fried rice, served in the rind

Price: $10 and under per person

Hours: Monday-Friday 11 a.m.-3 p.m., 5 p.m.-10 p.m.; Saturday-Sunday 12 p.m.-10 p.m.

La Fondue

Food: varied fondue dishes

14510 Big Basin Way

(408) 867-3332

Cool Features: alligator, ostritch, boar

Price: $60 and under per person

Hours: Monday-Thursday 5 p.m.-9:30 p.m.; Friday 5 p.m.-11 p.m., Saturday 4 p.m.-11 a.m., Sunday 4 p.m.-9:30 p.m.

Mango Cafe

Food: Jamaican

435 Hamilton Avenue

(650) 324-9443

Cool Features: goat, jerk chicken

Price: $15 and under per person

Hours: Monday-Thursday 6 p.m.-9:30 p.m., Friday-Saturday 6 p.m.-10 p.m., lunch on Fridays, 11:30 a.m.-2 p.m.

Max's Opera Cafe

Food: deli, variety

711 Stanford Shopping Center

(650) 323-6297

Cool Features: great sandwiches, '50s atmosphere

Price: $15 and under per person

Hours: Monday-Thursday 11:30 a.m.-9:30 p.m., Friday 11:30 a.m.-10:30 p.m., Saturday 11 a.m.-10:30 p.m., Sunday 11 a.m.-9 p.m.

Minokichi

Food: Japanese

150 University Avenue

(650) 324-9536

Cool Features: all-you-can-eat sushi

Price: $15 and under
per person

Hours: Daily, 11:30 a.m.-2:30 p.m., Sunday-Thursday 5:30 p.m.-10 p.m.

Miyake

Food: sushi

140 University Avenue

(650) 323-9449

Cool Features: Techno music, strobe lights (at night only)

Price: $25 and under
per person

Hours: Daily, 11:30 a.m.-10 p.m.

Osteria

Food: Italian

247 Hamilton Street

(650) 328-5700

Cool Features: excellent, authentic Tuscan cuisine

Price: $25 and under
per person

Hours: Monday-Friday 11:30 a.m.-2 p.m., Monday-Saturday 5 p.m.-10 p.m.

Pasta?

Food: Italian

326 University Avenue

(650) 328-4585

Cool Features: bruschetta

Price: $8 and under per person

Hours: Monday-Thursday 11:30 a.m.-11 p.m.; Friday-Saturday 11:30 a.m.-12.a.m.; Sunday 11:30 a.m.-10 p.m.

Peninsula Fountain & Grill (The Creamery)

Food: classic American diner

#2A in the Stanford Shopping Center, or
566 Emerson Street

(650) 327-3141

Cool Features: great milkshakes, though pricey at $4.95, and grilled cheese sandwiches

Price: $15 and under
per person
Hours: Monday-Saturday 8 a.m.-10 p.m.; Sunday 8 a.m.-9 p.m.

Pizza Chicago

Food: deep-dish pizza, pasta

4115 El Camino Real

(650) 424-9400

Cool Features: Try the Eddie Gaedel, a John Dillinger, or another specialty pizza.

Price: $10 and under
per person

Hours: Sunday-Thursday 11 a.m.-10 p.m.; Friday-Saturday 11 a.m.-11 p.m.

Pluto's

Food: salads, sandwiches

482 University Avenue
(650) 327-9569

Cool Features: yuppie dining at its best

Price: $10 and under
per person

Hours: Sunday-Thursday
11:30 a.m.-10 p.m.; Friday-Saturday 11 a.m.-11 p.m.

Zao Noodle Bar

Food: Asian "street" food

261 University Avenue
(650) 328-1988

Price: $12 and under
per person

Hours: Sunday-Thursday
11:30 a.m.-10 p.m.;
Friday-Saturday 11:30 a.m.-10:30 p.m.

Student Favorites:
Applewood Pizza
The Creamery
In-N-Out Burger
Pluto's

Late-Night Food:
Domino's delivers until 2 a.m.,
and In-N-Out until 1:30 a.m.,

24-Hour Eating:
Denny's
Jack in the Box
McDonald's

Closest Grocery Stores:
Safeway
325 S. Sharon Park
Menlo Park, CA 94025
(650) 854-3056

Trader Joe's
720 Menlo Avenue
Menlo Park, CA 94025
(650) 323-2134

Whole Foods Market
774 Emerson Street
Palo Alto, CA 94301
(650) 326-8676

Best Pizza:
Applewood Pizza,
Pizz'a Chicago

Best Chinese:
Fresh Taste
Hunan Garden

Best Breakfast:
Hobee's
Jack in the Box

Best Indian:
Janta

Best Healthy:
Trader Joe's
Whole Foods

Best Place to Take Your Parents:
The Fish Market

Students Speak Out On...
Off-Campus Dining

"Downtown Palo Alto has every variety of restaurant that you could ever want, but you kind of need a car to get to any of them."

Q "We have fast food places like Jack in the Box, and nicer stuff like Max's Opera Cafe. **Whatever your dining pleasure happens to be, it will be here somewhere**. I wouldn't say that there is any one definitive place to which everyone goes, but there are plenty of good places in the area."

Q "Off campus, we have Cold Stone for ice-cream and a bunch of **great ethnic restaurants—Japanese, Italian, and foods like that**—but many are expensive. So except for special occasions, or if you happen to find a nice, cheap little place, it's best to eat on campus."

Q "There's **pretty good food off University Avenue** and in Mountain View, which is a 20-minute drive away. Miyake is a popular Japanese restaurant, and Minokichi, across the street from campus, has an awesome buffet. The pasta around here is pretty good, and there are a bunch of good Chinese places, too."

Q "The Palo Alto restaurants tend to be pricey, but the **Thai places are good, and they are usually reasonably priced**. The only thing that we have in the way of a diner is Denny's or The Creamery—both of which I really like, but both of which are a little expensive."

Q "**Off-campus restaurants are incredibly nice**! Be prepared to spend some cash if you want to eat at the really fancy ones, though. There are plenty of restaurants that I go to that only cost $10 to $15 for a meal, and they're very, very nice! You won't need names of any restaurants since almost any place that you find downtown will be of high quality."

Q "**There are a lot of restaurants on University Avenue**, that you can get to by biking, driving, or the Marguerite [shuttle]. I personally eat a lot of Thai, so I'll recommend Krung Siam, which is one of the restaurants on University Avenue."

Q "**Pluto's is the best thing that ever happened to me**—great salads and meat that they cook right in front of you at very reasonable prices! Bella Luna and Osteria are great for taking your parents out. La Fondue in Saratoga has the best chocolate dessert fondue, which can be very romantic, too."

Q "**Palo Alto is the city of dining**. You'd think there might be slightly more culture in such a relatively affluent town, but apparently all the locals want to do is eat. There are all price ranges, all kinds of food, and most of them good. For Italian, try Pasta?—yes, it seriously comes with question mark—and Bella Luna."

Q "There are a lot of good restaurants off-campus, but I don't tend to eat out all that often. One of my favorite places is called Frankie, Johnnie, and Luigi Too! It's a great Italian place, with absolutely amazing knife-and-fork pizza. Order a 'Tina's Too-Too Much' for some serious eating. Given the size of the pizza, the prices are great. They also make excellent pastas and salads, for those who aren't in a pizza mood. The atmosphere is very casual, and **Stanford students get a 15 percent discount**. It's a good time all around."

The College Prowler Take On...
Off-Campus Dining

Palo Alto and its neighboring cities offer a great variety of dining options. Students are most pleased with the area's Asian food, including Indian, Thai, Chinese, and Japanese. In addition, there's plenty of good Italian and Mexican cuisine, and no shortage of fast food. Palo Alto is home to many expensive eateries that are only really appropriate if your parents are paying, but if you search around, you can find high-quality options in the $10 range, too. Stanford students really love to eat off campus and they will explore places in a large radius outside of Palo Alto. Student preferences vary considerably, but everyone seems to find something he or she likes that is budget-friendly.

Off-campus dining becomes a way of life for most Stanford students. For freshmen, it's a bit trickier since they can't have cars, but taking the Marguerite shuttle to downtown Palo Alto is a reasonable option. For upperclassmen, eating in the dining halls grows tiresome, and a meal off-campus provides a nice change of pace, and a chance to socialize. For upperclassmen living in Row houses—co-ops and self-ops—there are generally no meals on the weekend, so going off campus is essential. The cost of living in Silicon Valley is relatively high, so food can be expensive, but the student directory and Stanford newspaper usually have coupons.

The College Prowler® Grade on

Off-Campus
Dining: A

A high Off-Campus Dining grade implies that off-campus restaurants are affordable, accessible, and worth visiting. Other factors include the variety of cuisine and the availability of alternative options (vegetarian, vegan, Kosher, etc.).

Campus Housing

The Lowdown On...
Campus Housing

Room Types:
Singles
One or two-room doubles
One or two-room triples
One, two, or three-room quads

Best Dorms:
Lambda Nu, Xanada, BOB, 680
Lomita, other row houses

Worst Dorms:
Ethnic Theme Dorms, SLE
Dorms, Potter, Robinson,
Mirrielees

**Undergrads on
Campus:**
99%

**Number of
Dormitories/Houses:**
50

**Number of University-
Owned Apartments:**
None

→

All-Freshman Dorms:

Alondra, Cedro, Donner, Gavilan, Junipero, Larkin, Otero, Rinconada

Floors: 2-3

Total Occupancy: 60-95

Bathrooms: shared by floor

Coed: Yes

Percentage of First-Year Students: 100%

Room Types: one-room doubles

Special Features: lounge, grand piano, TV, DVD, VCR, ping pong, pool table, laundry

Branner

Floors: 3

Total Occupancy: 180

Bathrooms: shared by floor

Coed: Yes

Percentage of First-Year Students: 100%

Room Types: two-room triples

Special Features: lounge, grand piano, TV, DVD, VCR, ping pong, pool table, laundry

Four-Class Dorms:

Roble

Floors: 3

Total Occupancy: 310

Bathrooms: shared by floor

Coed: Yes

Percentage of First-Year Students: 55%

Room Types: singles, three-room quads (for freshmen)

(Roble, continued)

Special Features: lounge, grand piano, TV, DVD, VCR, ping pong, pool table, laundry

Freshman-Sophomore College (FroSoCo)

Floors: 3

Total Occupancy: 185

Bathrooms: shared by floor

Coed: Yes

Percentage of First-Year Students: 50%

Room Types: two-room doubles

Special Features: lounge, TV, DVD, pool, laundry, pool

Adelfa, Arroyo, Burbank, Casa Zapata*, Cardenal, Eucalipto, Faisan, Granada, Loro, Mirlo, Naranja, Okada*, Serra, Soto, Trancos, Twain, Ujamaa*, Muwekma-tah-ruk*

Floors: 2-3

Total Occupancy: 60-95

Bathrooms: shared by floor

Coed: Yes

Percentage of First-Year Students: 30%-50%

Room Types: one-room doubles

Special Features: lounge, grand piano, TV, DVD, VCR, ping pong, pool table, laundry

*Ethnic Theme houses:

Typically about half of the residents in these dorms identify with the house's ethnic theme. Casa Zapata is the Chicano/Latino theme

(Theme houses, continued)

dorm, Okada has an Asian focus, Ujamaa has an African American theme, and Muwekma-tah-ruk has a Native American emphasis.

Upperclass Housing:

Toyon

Floors: 3

Total Occupancy: 215

Bathrooms: shared by floor

Coed: Yes

Percentage of First-Year Students: 0% (all sophomores)

Room Types: two-room triples

Special Features: eating clubs, lounge, grand piano, TV, VCR, ping pong, pool, laundry

(Row Houses) 680 Lomita, 717 Dolores, Bob, Casa Italiana, Durand, EAST House, Grove Mayfield, Grove Lasuen, Haus Mitteleuropa, Lambda Nu, La Maison Francaise, Mars, Murray, Narnia, Phi Sig, Roth, Slav Dom, Storey, Xanadu, Yost, ZAP

Floors: 2-3

Total Occupancy: 30-65

Bathrooms: Shared by floor

Coed: Yes, except Roth, which is all-female

Percentage of First-Year Students: 0%

Room Types: singles, triples, doubles, quads

Special Features: With the exception of Yost and Murray,

(Row Houses, continued)

the houses are student run and managed. Students hire a chef who cooks about 10 meals a week for the house.

(Co-Ops) Chi Theta Chi, Columbae, Enchanted Broccoli Forest, Hammarsjköld, Kairos, Synergy, Terra

Floors: 2-3

Total Occupancy: 30-50

Bathrooms: shared by floor

Coed: Yes

Percentage of First-Year Students: 0%

Room Types: singles, triples, doubles, quads

Special Features: Students are fully responsible for planning meals, cooking, and cleaning all common areas.

Mirrielees

Floors: 4

Total Occupancy: 435

Bathrooms: shared by floor

Coed: Yes

Percentage of First-Year Students: 0%

Room Types: Apartment-style housing (doubles and singles)

Special Features: One of the few places on campus that doesn't require a meal plan. You have a kitchen and can make your own food.

Suites

Floors: 2-3

Total Occupancy: 250

Bathrooms: shared by suite

Coed: Yes (each suite is single sex)

Percentage of First-Year Students: 0%

Room Types: four or six-person suites

Special Features: Residents eat in one of several eating clubs.

Castaño, Lantana, Kimball, Potter, Robinson

Floors: 2-3

Total Occupancy: 90-200

Bathrooms: shared by floor
Coed: Yes

Percentage of First-Year Students: 0%

Room Types: two-room doubles

Special Features: quiet and study-oriented upper-class housing, lounge, grand piano, TV, DVD, VCR, ping pong, pool table, laundry

(Fraternities) Sigma Nu, Sigma Chi, Theta Delta Chi, Kappa Sigma, Sigma Alpha Epsilon, Phi Kappa Psi, Kappa Alpha

Floors: 2-3

Total Occupancy: 40-60

Bathrooms: shared by floor

Coed: men only

Percentage of First-Year Students: 0%

Room Types: two-room doubles

Special Features: They're fraternities, so there are lots of parties.

(Sororities) Delta Delta Delta, Pi Beta Phi, Kappa Alpha Theta

Floors: 2-3

Total Occupancy: 40-50

Bathrooms: shared by floor

Coed: women only

Percentage of First-Year Students: 0%

Room Types: two-room Doubles

Special Features: It's located right by Vaden, the student health center.

Bed Type
Twin extra-long (39x80"), some lofts, some bunk-beds

Available for Rent
Fridge, microwave, water dispenser

Cleaning Service?
Daily cleaning of bathrooms and common areas during the week in University housing. In co-ops, you get to do it yourself!

You Get
Bed, desk and chair, bookshelf, dresser, closet or wardrobe, window coverings, cable TV jack, Ethernet connection

Other Costs:
Internet: $10/month

Phone: $33 startup fee, $13 a month for local, 4-9 cents a minute for long-distance calls. If you have a roommate, you can share a phone and each pay half.

Did You Know?

Stanford, like the entire state of California, is **basically smoke-free**. You cannot smoke inside any restaurant, or even in bars.

Students Speak Out On...
Campus Housing

{ **"The dorms here are generally nicer than the dorms at most other universities. You can't avoid living in any particular dorm because you'll be a freshman, and freshmen are randomly placed into dormitories."**

Q "As a freshman, I would recommend that you **opt for an all-freshman dorm** because you get to know the most people that way, and it will also be more fun. I probably wouldn't do SLE (Structured Liberal Education) because you'll have a lot more work than the other freshman."

Q "Your freshman dorm room will be small. After that, you should use your good-room years during your sophomore and senior year, if possible, and try and draw into a Manzanita Park dorm, a Lagunita dorm, or Roble. Those three have many singles and two-room doubles, so you can have your own space. Also, if you have particular interests, or if you are a member of a particular ethnic group and you're willing to apply for it, **you can get priority housing**. So even if you get a bad number, you can still get into a good dorm."

Q "In general, **Stanford dorms are better than the dorms at most other colleges because they're roomier**. There are no particularly nice freshmen dorms except for Muwekma-Tah-Ruk (the Native-American themed house) and FroSoCo (Freshman-Sophomore College). You have to apply to get into either of them, and the social life there is kind of blah."

Q "The dorms are nice as far as dorms go. The Row houses are nice, too. **There's really no reason for you to avoid any of the dorms**."

Q "The dorms are pretty nice, and the people tend to be very cohesive. **You'll get to know the whole dorm pretty well; it's a good system**."

Q "As a freshman, **any all-freshman dorm is the best choice**. Upperclassmen prefer row houses, but all of the campus housing is good for the most part."

Q "Some dorms are nicer than others. I loved living in Lagunita Court, but those rooms are small, so consider yourself forewarned! The nice thing about having lived there is that after that year, which was my freshman year, every other place I lived in seemed really big. Freshman year, people usually want to live where all of the other freshmen are living, so you might want to live in an all-freshman dorm. **I personally loved living in a dorm with members of all four classes**. It's just a matter of personal preference."

Q "**Dorms are really sweet. Wilbur and Stern are the best**. Avoid FroSoCo—it's farthest from everything. FloMo is reasonable, but not as cool as Wilbur or Stern. Anything you get is pretty sweet, though."

Q "All the dorms are okay, but **avoid four-class dorms if you want a really social atmosphere as a freshman**. Conversely, if you are planning on getting some serious studying done freshman year, avoid all-freshman dorms, especially Branner."

Q "**Dorms are sort of like parachuting into an open field—you'll be fine wherever you land**. Some spots are better than others, like those houses on Mayfield Drive (a.k.a. "The Row"), but friendly faces abound most anywhere. The real problem with dorms is their ridiculous dispersion across this thousands-of-acres campus, making it a labor-intensive job to visit a friend in a dorm different from your own."

Q "Because almost everyone lives on campus, and housing is generally packed to maximum capacity, there is a distinct lack of singles. **I would say only about half of upperclassmen get their own room**. By senior year, this can be a real problem. Whether or not you have a single (or at least half of a two-room double) can have a very distinct effect on your social life."

The College Prowler Take On...
Campus Housing

Student opinions of on-campus housing are appropriately mixed—there are so many different options that your housing experience can vary. There are standard dormitories, with 60 to 200 people, self-operated houses, with 25 to 50 people, where students manage finances and hire a chef, and co-ops, where residents do all of the cooking and cleaning. Mirrielees is an apartment-style dorm where you don't have a meal plan, and you can do your own cooking. Some students are quite happy living in a regular dormitory, while others have a much better time in a smaller house. Most feel that freshman year is best spent living in an all-freshman dorm, because you'll get to know a lot more people and have a better social life. After freshman year, you have the option to live in a dorm again, or in a Row house. Stanford's lottery system, called "The Draw," has a huge effect on the options you have each year.

Stanford definitely has one of the most diverse housing systems of any university, and there's a large disparity between the qualities of different options. Some students live in crowded one-room triples and have mediocre food, while others live in singles and have a great house chef. The lottery, which gives you a random number that affects where you can live, supposedly mediates the disparity. Of course, some people are just unlucky. Others will manage to find loopholes. Some people join fraternities, while others become staff members. Where you live on campus greatly influences your quality of life, though not always for the most obvious reasons. Having good food or a large room is nice, but sometimes having the right roommate or good people in your hall makes the biggest difference.

B+

The College Prowler® Grade on
Campus Housing: B+

A high Campus Housing grade indicates that dorms are clean, well-maintained, and spacious. Other determining factors include variety of dorms, proximity to classes, and social atmosphere.

Off-Campus Housing

The Lowdown On...
Off-Campus Housing

Undergrads in Off-Campus Housing:
1%

Average Rent For:
1BR Apt.: $1,607
Studio Apt.: $700

Popular Areas:
Within Palo Alto: Town & Country area;
Outside: Portola Valley, Redwood City, Mountainview

Best Time to Look for a Place:
Spring

For Assistance Contact:
www.stanford.edu/dept/hds/chs/
(650) 723-3906
communityhousing@lists.stanford.edu

Students Speak Out On...
Off-Campus Housing

"I don't live on campus, but the vast majority of Stanford students do because Palo Alto is one of the most expensive areas in which to live in the entire nation."

Q "**You won't be living off campus**; Palo Alto houses cost about 10 times more than other houses. You'll probably live on campus for all four years (which isn't bad because you can live in houses on campus). Most of the students here live on campus."

Q "**Nobody really lives off campus here**. It's way too expensive in Palo Alto. On-campus housing options are better than those at most other schools, anyway."

Q "**Living off campus can be expensive** (though it's been cheaper than usual recently), but there are free shuttles that run all over campus, and to the public train stations and such. So, depending on how close you are to a shuttle stop or a train station, living off campus can be convenient."

Q "**The off-campus housing situation is bad**. Palo Alto is ridiculously expensive. Stanford guarantees its students four years of housing, so about 90 percent of students live on campus for all four years."

Q "You can find places to live in the area around Stanford, but they're very expensive. **There's no real reason to live off campus**."

Q "**No one lives off campus** because the property around Stanford is very expensive, and we are guaranteed on-campus housing."

Q "Housing is **very inconvenient, unless you are rich and have a car**. Remember, the campus is large, and the nearest place is downtown Palo Alto. You figure it out."

Q "No one lives off campus. **It's too expensive and too inconvenient**."

Q "I never even considered it. It can be cheaper, but it's a pain to bike onto campus, and you can't really get a parking permit unless you live on campus or want to pay a lot of money. **The Dead Houses are the best off-campus option** for many because they're close, they have DSL, and they have a co-op environment, where you cook for yourself and live with a group of people."

Q "**Don't even think about moving off campus**. You'll miss a large part of the social scene, plus however many thousands you spend on your tiny Silicon Valley room."

Q "The campus is big, which means that commuting from an off-campus apartment to class can be a bit of a pain. Real estate is also exceedingly expensive in the Palo Alto area, so **finding a room with a reasonable rent can be rather difficult**. Some folks really seem to enjoy being away from campus for a bit, but overall, I'd recommend sticking with an on-campus residence."

The College Prowler Take On...
Off-Campus Housing

The majority of students are unified in the opinion that off-campus housing is a bad idea. It is universally considered too expensive and inconvenient (given the enormous and isolated campus). It's also true that living off campus almost definitely requires a car. Since Stanford guarantees four years of on-campus housing, few are willing to accept the cost and trouble of living on their own.

Despite all the negative opinions about off-campus housing, however, it can be done. For students who are tired of the Stanford social scene, living off campus is the only way to get out of the "Stanford Camp" environment and more into the real world. If you split renting a house with several friends, rent could be around $500 a month, which is comparable to what you pay for a room on-campus. If off-campus life seems like an attractive idea, it's best to start looking early for both roommates and living space; both of these are limited around Stanford, so finding the means to move off campus can turn into a serious project.

D-

The College Prowler® Grade on
Off-Campus
Housing: D-

A high grade in Off-Campus Housing indicates that apartments are of high quality, close to campus, affordable, and easy to secure.

Diversity

The Lowdown On...
Diversity

Native American:
2%

White:
45%

Asian American:
24%

International:
6%

African American:
11%

Unknown:
None

Hispanic:
12%

Out-of-State:
53%

Political Activity

Most students identify as left/liberal or apathetic. There are relatively few protests, though a few professors and students will put together occasional rallies for or against various political issues. Despite the overwhelming liberal tendencies, there is actually an active pocket of budding young republicans, who get moral support from the Hoover Institute—a conservative academic group on campus.

Gay Pride

The campus and surrounding communities are highly accepting of gay students. There are support groups on campus, such as QSSPA and the LBTCRC. The gay community is relatively visible within Stanford. There are gay parties, and one co-op unofficially serves as a center for gay students who want to live together.

Economic Status

Stanford certainly makes an effort to diversify, not only in racial and ethnic terms, but also with regard to economic status. There are some very poor students here, but also some extremely rich ones. Your average Stanford student is upper-middle-class.

Minority Clubs

Most minorities at Stanford have some form of a community center, and many associated clubs. There are ethnic Greek organizations, including African American, Chicano, Jewish, and Asian fraternities.

Most Popular Religions

Christianity (Protestant and Catholic), Judaism

Students Speak Out On...
Diversity

> **"I think what really stuck in my mind when I visited Stanford was how culturally diverse the place was. I saw people from many different backgrounds working together."**

Q "**This campus is surprisingly diverse**. My friends here are Colombian, Lebanese, South African, Asian, and African American. I am white. It's pretty cool and pretty diverse here."

Q "**Diversity is a big deal on campus**. Various student ethnic organizations—Asian, Latino, black—are active and very involved politically on campus from what I've observed in the past."

Q "It's very diverse, but **the diversity seems to be primarily Asian and non-Asian** as opposed to white and non-white."

Q "It's getting more and more diverse every year. I think that **less than 50 percent of students are white**."

Q "**There are ethnic themed houses**—whether that helps or hurts diversity is something for you to decide."

Q "**The campus is ethnically and religiously diverse**, but I'd say there is a fair amount of segregation along those lines. Ethnically-themed houses tend to encourage this, but I don't think segregation is a hugely destructive force on our campus."

Q **"The campus is diverse, but cultural groups don't really mix**. People who want to be involved in their cultural group tend to stick with it, live in a cultural theme house, and not mingle with other groups."

Q "Campus is very diverse, with non-Hispanic Caucasians making up less than 50 percent of the campus population. **Groups do tend to mix, though people are more likely to hang out with folks of their own race**. The campus culture is very tolerant and open, but be prepared to play by the standard rules of political correctness. Despite the significant diversity on campus, there is considerable complaining by some students about the lack of it. Be prepared for some sort of newspaper article bemoaning the lack of diversity on campus every day."

Q "It's been pretty good. My freshman year, I lived with about 90 people, and basically every roommate pair in our dorm was comprised of **two people of different races**. Expect to live with someone very different from you freshman year."

The College Prowler Take On...
Diversity

Both the diversity statistics and the students' perspectives plainly show that Stanford is a diverse university. The student body is less than half Caucasian, and includes many international students. African Americans and Hispanics, two typical minority groups, comprise approximately 20 percent of the undergraduate student body. Stanford is able to achieve this level of diversity through its belief in affirmative action. However, racial diversity is not the only concern for Stanford. It also achieves diversity by attracting students interested in a broad range of academic fields, from the humanities to engineering, as well as some of the nation's best athletes. Most students are very happy with this level of diversity. Some, however, admit that although there is ethnic diversity, racial groups still tend to remain segregated.

For several years in a row, Stanford has released reports in the spring announcing that it has admitted the "most diverse class ever" based on the increasing percentage of minority students. Students are receptive to the growing diversity, and many have been impressed by the cultural representation across campus. The system of ethnic theme houses does have the potential for isolation, but this is generally outweighed by the positive aspects of the system; Stanford will likely expose you to more diverse people and cultures than you've ever encountered.

The College Prowler® Grade on
Diversity: A

A high grade in Diversity indicates that ethnic minorities and international students have a notable presence on campus and that students of different economic backgrounds, religious beliefs, and sexual preferences are well-represented.

Guys & Girls

The Lowdown On...
Guys & Girls

Men Undergrads:
52%

Women Undergrads:
48%

Birth Control Available?
Birth Control pills are subsidized by Vaden, the student health center, for $9 a month. The SHPRC (Sexual Health Peer Resource Center) sells a wide array of contraceptives at heavily discounted prices. All undergrads can get 12 free condoms per quarter.

Most Prevalent STDs on Campus
Herpes, Chlamydia, HPV (Genital Warts)

Hookups or Relationships?

Stanford tends to have a good deal of hookups, but probably no more than at other colleges or universities. Hookups are more common than casual dating, for the most part, because of Stanford students' busy schedules and constant workloads.

Best Place to Meet Guys/Girls

You are likely to meet a potential boyfriend/girlfriend in class, through friends, or at a party. Every couple at Stanford tends to have a pretty unique story. Frat parties aren't great for meeting people—smaller, quieter house parties are more conducive to meeting and talking with others. Some students are quick to point out the critical timing required by the quarter system. For the first couple weeks, everyone wants to have fun, and many may end up in various romantic situations. By the middle and end of the quarter, most students are so bogged down with work that they let their social lives slip away.

Social Scene

The social scene has as much variety as the range of people on campus. The more academic students, who spend a lot of time studying, don't make much of an effort to date. Many students bemoan the lack of dating at Stanford, and simultaneously spend the majority of their time in the library studying. The social students often join fraternities or sororities because they want a steady supply of parties and other gatherings. But even outside of Greek life, the Stanford residential system is quite conducive to meeting people because there are always group activities that get people out of their rooms. What people choose to make of these opportunities is really just a matter of personal priority.

Did You Know?

Top Three Places to Find Hotties:
1. Frat parties
2. The Oval in spring
3. Dance/yoga classes

Top Places to Hook Up:
1. Frats
2. In your room, if you have a single
3. Psychology building roof
4. History Corner basement
5. The Dish

Dress Code

The dress standard is extremely casual. Most of the year, students wear flip-flops and T-shirts. Students wake up and go right to class, wearing whatever. If you hang out with the co-op crowd, people might not even bother to wear shoes at all. But Stanford students can look nice from time to time. If there's an official dance or formal social event, students will wear nice clothes for a refreshing change.

Students Speak Out On...
Guys & Girls

"Surprisingly, there are a lot of hot girls here. Everyone seems pretty cool."

Q "I have a lot of attractive guy friends, and a lot of people have also made this observation. **A lot of the girls complain that the guys don't take the initiative**. It's kind of hard to date here, but plenty of people do."

Q "There are cute guys and girls obviously, and then there are not-so-cute guys and girls. **Stanford guys joke about how all of the Stanford girls are ugly**, which certainly isn't true, but I can't tell either way."

Q "The consensus seems to be that **Stanford guys are pretty good-looking**, and Stanford girls are not."

Q "They say that **Stanford girls are busted**, and that the dudes are really hot and Californian, but I think it's the other way around."

Q "We have some ugly ones and some hot ones on both sides. **Most people tend to be friendly**. Lots of people just want to be the best, but that is hard to avoid at a school such as this one."

Q "**Most people are attractive**, though it is a very academically-oriented school."

Q "**Don't come here for the girls**. Stay here long enough and your standards will take a nosedive, also known as getting 'Stanford glasses.'"

Q "I'm from Hawaii, so I tend to like my Hawaii boys the most, but **there are a lot of cuties here**, too! Stanford people are usually really nice because it's more laid-back here than at most other colleges, I think. Of course, sometimes you'll run into the punks and jerks, but you'll find that anywhere you go."

Q "Guys here are better than girls when it comes to having good looks. **Stanford doesn't have the best reputation in terms of good-looking people**, but after a while, you tend to find everybody attractive, simply because you spend so much time with them."

Q "From a guy's perspective, I've found that the number of attractive girls at this school isn't on par with most others. **Apparently the athletes are the most attractive people on campus**, but I'm making this observation with as little personal bias as possible."

Q "Well, not too many people really date. But everyone can definitely find people for their own tastes here. **Random hookups are the way it happens here**."

Q "The guys fall into three categories: the taken, the untouchables (it's a shame that the engineering department is so big here), and the acceptable ones that are impossible to find. More than half of the guys in my freshman dorm came to Stanford **still together with their high school girlfriends**."

Q "As far as guys vs. girls, I'd say that the girls here are better, simply because there are fewer girls who do engineering. This said, **I happened to find myself quite a catch in the CS department**, but I didn't find him until almost halfway through my senior year, if that gives you any idea about the selection here."

Q "It is rumored that many years ago, a magazine declared Stanford to have the 'ugliest girls' of any college campus. Lately, however, the consensus is that the girls get better looking every year. My verdict would be that **Stanford kids are generally the slightly nerdy, to quite nerdy,** laid-back, and down-to-earth type, that is, if they can fit a particular type at all."

The College Prowler Take On...
Guys & Girls

The level of attractiveness at Stanford is definitely up for debate. Many students feel that the Stanford population is reasonably good-looking. However, a lot of students, particularly the male ones, will express the controversial opinion that at Stanford the guys are hot, and the girls are not. Students of both sexes in engineering majors have a particularly bad reputation for being awkward and unattractive. Dating at Stanford can be tricky, because many students feel the need to put so much time into their studies. If you come to Stanford as a slightly awkward overachiever and you don't make the effort to meet girls or guys, you definitely won't.

There is a lot of going steady and less casual dating, but there is also a hookup culture, about equal to the amount of steady relationships. People who are more into casual dating tend to join fraternities and sororities. Given the good weather and athletic culture of the school, there's definitely a general concern for physical fitness. This often translates to some hard bodies, but the faces can't quite stack up. Most of the students were nerds in high school, after all, and the ineptness in the social scene has, not surprisingly, carried over into higher education.

**The College Prowler® Grade on
Guys: B+**

A high grade for Guys indicates that the male population on campus is attractive, smart, friendly, and engaging, and that the school has a decent ratio of guys to girls.

**The College Prowler® Grade on
Girls: B-**

A high grade for Girls not only implies that the women on campus are attractive, smart, friendly, and engaging, but also that there is a fair ratio of girls to guys.

Athletics

The Lowdown On...
Athletics

Athletic Division:
NCAA Division I

Conference:
Pacific 10 Conference

School Mascot:

Stanford's official mascot is Cardinal—not the bird, but the color. And the color is represented by the highly-touted and nationally-renowned "Tree."

Number of Males Playing Varsity Sports:
433 (13%)

Number of Females Playing Varsity Sports:
388 (12%)

➜

Men's Varsity Sports:
Baseball
Basketball
Crew
Cross-Country
Fencing
Football
Golf
Gymnastics
Sailing
Soccer
Swimming/Diving
Tennis
Track & Field
Volleyball
Water Polo
Wrestling

Women's Varsity Sports:
Basketball
Crew
Cross-Country
Fencing
Field Hockey
Golf
Gymnastics
Lacrosse
Sailing
Soccer
Softball
Swimming/Diving
Synchronized Swimming
Tennis
Track & Field
Volleyball
Water Polo

Club Sports:
Badminton
Climbing Wall
Cycling
Ice Hockey
Men's Lacrosse
Polo
Men's Rugby
Women's Rugby
Running
Ski Team
Tae Kwon Do
Ultimate Frisbee

Intramurals:
Badminton
Basketball
Billiards
Dodgeball
Foosball
Kickball
Soccer
Softball
Table Tennis
Tennis
Ultimate Frisbee
Volleyball

Getting Tickets

Tickets are generally easy to get if you are a student. For the big sports like basketball or football, you'll have to buy season passes, but they are usually very reasonable—around $50. Less popular sports, like volleyball, have very cheap tickets, and some sports, including gymnastics and lacrosse, tend to be free for Stanford students.

Fields/Facilities

Artificial turf field
Avery Aquatic Center
Boyd & Jill Smith Family Stadium
Burnham Pavilion
Cobb Track & Angell Field
Maloney Field
Maples Pavilion
Morrison Boathouse
Stanford Golf Course
Stanford Stadium
Sunken Diamond
Taube Family Tennis Center

Most Popular Sports

Men's basketball and football, and women's basketball are the most popular events, by far. Students seem to really enjoy volleyball games, as well as attending track & field meets.

Best Place to Take a Walk

Arboretum Road is a nice place to take a walk, and it runs straight through most of Stanford's athletic facilities.

Students Speak Out On...
Athletics

"Athletics are very big here. The sports teams are really good. A lot of people who aren't that good play IM sports."

Q "**Varsity sports at Stanford are probably the best in the world** at the collegiate level. IM sports are fun, and very big, as well."

Q "**Sports dominate Stanford**. That's definitely a theme that brings everybody together. IM sports are awesome too, which is definitely a plus."

Q "**Varsity sports are pretty big here** because we do so well in them, especially in women's sports. Intramural sports are also pretty big, and they are there if you want to participate in them. We have a fair amount of Olympic athletes here, and all that, which is pretty cool."

Q "Varsity and IM sports are both pretty big here, but **varsity sports are particularly big**. My family and friends are local, so I'm off campus too much to participate in sports very much, but Stanford offers classes for volleyball, and many other sports (though no basketball class, to my dismay), so even if you can't play in an IM sport, you can still find athletic activities in which to take part."

Q "IM sports are pretty big. In terms of student enthusiasm, **we have our fair share of hardcore fans**."

Q "Lots of students follow and support varsity sports, and **we have incredible varsity teams**. IM sports are very popular among students—ultimate Frisbee and Frisbee golf in particular."

Q "**Varsity sports here are huge**, and the IM sports are what you make of them."

Q "We won the NACAD Directors' Cup [formerly the Sears Directors' Cup] for the best college athletics program in the nation in 2003, so **our varsity sports are pretty big-time**. Athletes don't usually get any special recognition from the student body like they might at other schools, though. IM sports are pretty big. Some people take them very seriously, but they are a lot of fun."

Q "Sports are a pretty big deal at Stanford. The size of the school, however, is not proportional to our teams' excellence. **Football and basketball are both pretty popular**, but if there are midterms, attendance at games will be way down. There are a lot of IM sports, and anyone who wants to get involved in them can definitely find a team to play on."

Q "We have the best athletic program in the nation, but most people **only recognize us for our academics**."

Q "For a school that dominates in so many sports, **there's relatively little student support**. Except for basketball; everyone loves basketball here. IM sports are always fun, and a lot of people participate."

Q "Varsity sports are huge, since **Stanford is such an athletic powerhouse**. Stanford is home to many world-class athletes, which makes attending sports events even more exciting."

The College Prowler Take On...
Athletics

Stanford really does have one of the nation's best overall athletic programs and manages to excel in everything from swimming to fencing. Everyone seems to be quite aware of the school's success, and it is a matter of pride for most students. Still, Stanford teams are not supported by the student body to the extent that other comparable college athletics are. Students are often just too busy to get out and watch many of the games. If a team is having a poor season, game attendance will be especially dismal. Students are really into intramural sports, however. If someone wants to play a sport in a semi-organized way, it is definitely possible; and even if you don't play on an official IM team, there are always a lot of pick-up basketball, soccer, or ultimate frisbee games.

Having so many athletes at Stanford adds a strange dimension to what is generally considered a primarily academic institution. It may be interesting to have an IHUM section with future Olympic athletes, but don't be surprised when you learn that many of them scored in the 1000 range on the SAT. Still, some athletes are among the best students at Stanford, and manage to excel across the board. If you don't play a sport, there is no better institution at which to be a fan—there is always a winning team at Stanford to cheer for.

The College Prowler® Grade on

Athletics: A

A high grade in Athletics indicates that students have school spirit, that sports programs are respected, that games are well-attended, and that intramurals are a prominent part of student life.

Nightlife

The Lowdown On...
Nightlife

Club and Bar Prowler: Popular Nightlife Spots!

Club Crawler:

There are only a couple of clubs right around campus. Students don't visit them very often, but once in a while, it can be fun. For more serious clubbers, San Francisco is the way to go.

The Edge
260 S. California Avenue
(650) 321-6464
http://theedge.club.net/info.html
The Edge features hip-hop and house, and occasional live bands, which have included acts such as Alien Ant Farm. It's 21 and over, except on Tuesdays.

Q Cafe
529 Alma Street
(650) 322-3311
*http://www.themenupage.
com/Qcafe.html*
Depending on the day of the
week, Q features hip-hop,
house, or Top 40 music. Q also
has several pool tables and
occasional live music.

Oakland and San Francisco Clubs:

1015 Folsom
1015 Folsom Street,
San Francisco
(415) 431-1200
http://www.1015.com
A very popular nightclub with
multiple levels and rooms,
1015 features celebrity DJs
and is right in the middle of
the SOMA (South of Market)
club scene.

DNA Lounge
375 Eleventh Street,
San Francisco
http://www.dnalounge.com
(415) 626-1409
One of SF's more colorful
night scenes, DNA Lounge
features electronic music,
wild lights and visual
displays, and fluorescently
costumed dancers.

Yoshi's
510 Embarcadero West,
Jack London Square, Oakland
http://www.yoshis.com/
(510) 238-9200
Yoshi's features world-class,
live jazz performances. Come
early and eat some sushi at the
adjoining Japanese restaurant.

Bar Prowler:

Antonio's Nuthouse
321 California Avenue
(650) 321-2550
The Nuthouse is dark and
somewhat dirty, with peanut
shells all over the floor. It has
pool and a jukebox and now
serves decent Mexican food.

Compadres
3877 El Camino Real
(650) 858-1141
Both a nightspot and
a Mexican restaurant,
Compadres offers good food,
great margaritas, and an
enjoyable view from its patio.

Blue Chalk Cafe
630 Ramona Street
(650) 326-1020
A downtown favorite, Blue
Chalk features pool, darts,
videos, and Southern cooking.

The Dutch Goose
3567 Alameda De Las Pulgas
(650) 854-3245
Another dimly-lit bar with the
names of Stanford students
carved into every table. Try the
deviled eggs.

The Oasis Beer Garden
241 El Camino Real
(650) 326-8896
The Oasis has cheap pitchers
and features great food, like
hamburgers and pizza.

The Old Pro's
2865 El Camino Real
(650) 325-2070
One of a few sports bars in the
area, Old Pro's has reasonably
priced beer and lots of TVs.

Student Favorites:

Antonio's Nuthouse,
Blue Chalk, The Dutch Goose,
The Oasis Beer Garden,

Useful Resources for Nightlife:

http://unofficial.stanford.edu
(Go to "explore the guide,"
and choose "A Night on the
Town" from the drop-down
menu.)

Bars Close At:

2 a.m.

Local Specialties:

Pyramid, Sierra Nevada

Primary Areas with Nightlife:

In Palo Alto, the bars are
scattered all over. In San
Francisco, the best places are
in SOMA, the Mission, or the
Haight.

Other Places to Check Out:

British Bankers Club, Fanny
and Alexander, The Island,
The Rose and Crown,

Favorite Drinking Games:

Beer Pong, Card Games,
Century Club, Power Hour,
Quarters

What to Do if You're Under 21

Campus parties are your best bet. Expect to find something going
on at a fraternity or row house on most Fridays and Saturdays.
There are occasional Thursday parties, and EBF has happy hour
every week on Wednesday featuring music and kegs.

Students Speak Out On...
Nightlife

"There are some bars around here. A lot of people go to San Francisco and have really good times there, but there is plenty to do in the Stanford party scene. I was surprised when I got here."

Q "San Francisco is great, but it's hard to get there as a freshman because freshmen can't have cars."

Q "Most of the partying takes place on campus, though I've heard of a few places where people go to party off campus like Compadres."

Q "I think you have to be 21 to get into the bars. I don't know of any good ones, but I know that there is a tradition called Senior Pub Night where all of the seniors go to various bars on Thursday nights."

Q "Parties on campus tend to not last past 2 a.m., which sucks. However, they're pretty good for free parties."

Q "On-campus parties are great. The administration has a very trusting and laid-back alcohol policy. Frats can be pretty bad, but there's usually a really cool house party every weekend. There's not really a big off-campus bar scene."

Q "**After freshman year, many people stop attending huge parties** and go more for private room parties with their friends, going off campus to Palo Alto or San Francisco, and finding more alternatives to drinking."

Q "What's off-campus? Rarely do people venture down Palm Drive, unless it's for **a school organized 'Pub Night**.' Parties on campus include those given by dorms and fraternities, the latter trumping the former, should the two occur together. Stanford parties are about thoroughly enjoying a time when you're not working with the people that make campus so stellar; it's not about hitting up eight frat houses in a row."

The College Prowler Take On...
Nightlife

Like much of the Stanford experience, nightlife also revolves around on-campus activities. Students are more likely to spend a Friday or Saturday at a campus party than at a bar. There are generally a lot of campus parties, both at fraternities and dorms. Students also hold private parties in their own rooms or in dorm common areas. Upperclassmen may go to off-campus bars, to some extent; but given the location of these bars, a car and a designated driver are both necessary. Every year, the senior class arranges to have the campus shuttles take seniors to a different bar each Thursday night. This allows seniors to discover the local bar scene a bit more, though in the somewhat unusual context of 50 to 100 classmates. There are a few clubs in the Palo Alto area that are popular with students, but clubbing in San Francisco is more prominent. However, given that the city is an hour away, logistics can pose a problem.

In general, students are fairly satisfied with on-campus nightlife. With a variety of houses and students, there are many different types of parties. Every Wednesday night, EBF [Enchanted Broccoli Forest] holds happy hour, featuring beer and a DJ or live music. Almost every weekend, there is some sort of frat party, often with an interesting theme. A few times each quarter, the French theme house holds Café Nights, featuring wine, desserts, and live jazz. Whether you live in a dorm or a Row house, you will almost certainly hold your own parties with your friends a few times a year.

The College Prowler® Grade on

Nightlife: B

A high grade in Nightlife indicates that there are many bars and clubs in the area that are easily accessible and affordable. Other determining factors include the number of options for the under-21 crowd and the prevalence of house parties.

Greek Life

The Lowdown On...
Greek Life

Number of Fraternities:
15 (7 housed)

Number of Sororities:
11 (3 housed)

Undergrads Men in Fraternites:
13%

Undergrads Women in Sororities:
12%

Housed Fraternities on Campus:

Kappa Alpha
Kappa Sigma
Phi Kappa Psi
Sigma Alpha Epsilon
Sigma Chi
Sigma Nu
Theta Delta Chi

Un-Housed Fraternities on Campus:

Alpha Epsilon Pi
Alpha Pi Alpha
Delta Kappa Epsilon
Delta Tau Delta
Gamma Zeta Alpha
Kappa Alpha Psi
Lambda Phi Epsilon
Sigma Phi Epsilon

Housed Sororities on Campus:

Delta Delta Delta
Kappa Alpha Theta
Pi Beta Phi

Un-Housed Sororities on Campus:

Alpha Kappa Alpha
Chi Omega Kappa
Delta Sigma Tau
Kappa Delta Phi
Kappa Gamma
Lambda Theta Nu
Sigma Psi Zeta
Sigma Theta Psi

Other Greek Organizations:

Greek Council
Interfraternity Council
Intersorority Council

Students Speak Out On...
Greek Life

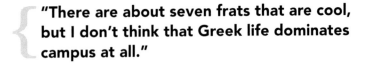

{ **"There are about seven frats that are cool, but I don't think that Greek life dominates campus at all."**

Q "**Greek life dominates when it comes to parties**. There are a lot of sororities and fraternities on campus. Parties at Greek houses are usually open to all Stanford students —uncommon at some schools—but some parties are invite-only. We have a very good party scene; there's usually stuff going on every weekend."

Q "Greek life shows up here and there on campus, but parties and the social scene are definitely not controlled by the sororities and fraternities. **I've never been to many frat parties, and I'm not in a sorority**."

Q "**Greek life is there**, but it does not take over the social scene, because most of the fraternities and sororities don't have houses."

Q "It is my my social scene because I'm really involved with my sorority, and my guy friends are mostly in fraternities, but it doesn't have to be the center of anyone's life. **Only about 10 to15 percent of the campus is involved with Greek life**."

Q "The Greek scene is not very big. There are fraternity parties and stuff, but **nobody takes Greek life that seriously**. It is there if you want it, though, and it's not that exclusive."

Q "It definitely doesn't take over social life, though **the fraternities throw the most parties**."

Q **"There is definitely Greek life on this campus, but it's not the only social scene**. The fraternities are usually the places that throw the most campus parties, but it's not like that's the only thing you can do if you want to have fun. What I found amazing about Stanford is the abundance of different things that you can do to have a good time. I'm not kidding. Anything that you can think of that you might want to do probably already has a place on campus."

Q "Greek life is pretty low-key. Stanford has very few housed fraternities and sororities, and usually **Greek parties are not exclusive to Greek members**, which means everyone can enjoy a good frat party. It definitely does not control the social scene."

Q "Ask people what they think about Greek life here, and you'll most likely get a shrug. **Fraternities and sororities are not extreme**, so the student body reaction to them is generally just as lukewarm. They provide good parties and are generally well behaved, but since less than 15 percent of students participate in them, it's hard to say whether the Greek system would shrink or expand your social horizon."

Q **"If you want it, it's there, if you don't, no worries**. Greeks make up a small but significant portion of the student body. Though most everyone will go to a few frat parties, Greek culture is not monolithic, and there is no real need to join a frat or sorority."

Q "I wouldn't say that the fraternities make up the entire the social scene—you don't have to be in one in order to have fun. I am not in one, and I have tight group of friends. But I will be honest with you, there are a lot of really nerdy or socially awkward kids here. It's because they are so darn smart, that they don't know how to socialize. Other than that, **you have the fraternity guys who seem to get a lot of the girls**—I hope I don't sound too bitter about that. If you like to party, fraternities throw good ones. If you don't, there's plenty of other stuff to do."

Q "**Every weekend there's something** Greek going on."

Q "**You make your own social scene here**. If you want to avoid the Greek scene, there are plenty of people, myself included, who will laugh at them along with you. If you want to make it part of your scene, about 15 percent of students are involved with it."

Q "Greek life is pretty big here; the **fraternities have most of the parties**. Sororities aren't as big."

Q "Only about 15 percent of the Stanford Student Body is Greek. Some of the fraternities, like Kappa Sig, Theta Delta and Sigma Chi, throw a good number of parties, when not on probation. **The rest of them just hog prime housing on campus**. Stanford is one of the few universities that actually encourages Greek participation by taking housing away from Independents in order to house its fraternities and sororities. Most members of the Greek system at Stanford say they enjoy the camaraderie and social scene, but admit that the Greeks at Stanford are nowhere near as 'hardcore' or 'gung-ho' as their state school counterparts."

Q "The on-campus social scene is generally pretty lively. Parties are held by fraternities, independent houses, and dorms—even ones that exclusively house freshmen. This speaks to Stanford's relatively laid-back drinking policy. Each weekend, there is usually one big party, and several smaller ones. **Notable mentions include Theta Chi's 'Glitter Party,' and Kappa Sig's 'Luau.'**"

The College Prowler Take On...
Greek Life

Most students agree that fraternities and sororities don't dominate Stanford's social scene. Fraternities sponsor the majority of popular parties on campus, but these are generally open to all students, and there are plenty of alternatives. A large majority of students don't feel the need to participate in Greek life at all, and most feel that the current size of Stanford's Greek system is large enough, if not too big. At a school with less than 15 percent of students going Greek, that sentiment is telling. If you don't rush, you will still be able to have plenty of fun and make friends as an undergraduate.

The Greek system at Stanford is fairly diverse. There's a frat for computer enthusiasts who like to play computer games over the LAN. There are some more traditional ones that are mainly comprised of athletes. There's even an anti-frat fraternity where most of the guys are into playing guitar and being laid-back. Still another frat tends to center around networking and being in student government. The sororities don't have as much diversity, but do break down roughly by a combination of attractiveness and sexual discretion. For students who want to get involved in Greek life but don't want as much of a commitment, there are several un-housed frats and sororities.

The College Prowler® Grade on

Greek Life: B-

A high grade in Greek Life indicates that sororities and fraternities are not only present, but also active on campus. Other determining factors include the variety of houses available and the respect the Greek community receives from the rest of the campus.

Drug Scene

The Lowdown On...
Drug Scene

Most Prevalent Drugs on Campus:

Alcohol, marijuana

Liquor-Related Referrals:

0

Liquor-Related Arrests:

87 for MIP/Drunken Behaviors
56 for DWI

Drug-Related Referrals:

0

Drug-Related Arrests:

13 for Possession

Drug Counseling Programs

Alcohol, Tobacco, and Other Drug Abuse Prevention Programs
http://vaden.stanford.edu/topics_resources/drug_use
(650) 723-3429
E-mail: rjcastro@stanford.edu
Services: education, seminars, individual consultation, written
and online resources, and referral information

Counseling and Psychological Services (CAPS)
http://vaden.stanford.edu/caps
(650) 723-3785
Services: assessment and treatment for drug abuse

Students Speak Out On...
Drug Scene

"I can assure you that the presence of drugs is very limited due to the stringent academic requirements of this school. You'd have to cross the Bay and go to Berkeley to find that sort of 'scene.'"

Q "I've seen people smoke pot, but there isn't much more than that on this campus. **I'm not saying that there isn't more going on, but I don't see it**. "

Q "I never notice much of a drug scene. **I know there are certain dorms that have a reputation, or at least one dorm in particular does**. But even so, I don't think it's that big."

Q "I wouldn't know much about the drug scene personally, except that it's there. **If you take the time to look, then drugs are not hard to find**."

Q "People smoke pot, but it's not that big. **Most people stick with alcohol**."

Q "Drug use is pretty minimal. **Some people smoke pot, but harder drugs are pretty rare on campus**. Relatively few people smoke cigarettes. People drink, but no more than at any other university."

Q "I think that there's a lot of weed on campus, but it's not like you'll be faced with it if you don't want to be faced with it. **It depends on who you hang with and stuff**. Also, there's no pressure on you to do something if you don't want to."

Q "The only drugs that I see at all on campus are alcohol and marijuana, **but those aren't a big issue** because it's not like people isolate you if you do, or don't, use them."

Q "Weed is the **only drug that's in common use**."

Q "Drugs are really not that big here; it's kind of surprising that for a laid-back California school we don't have a lot more people who smoke marijuana regularly. That is not to say that people here don't do recreational drugs, but **the drug culture is definitely not pronounced**, and the use of hardcore drugs is rare."

Q "From what I can tell, hard drug use is quite rare. **Marijuana, however, is extremely common**. Within the dorms, you're not really at risk of arrest. Drinking is even more common."

The College Prowler Take On...
Drug Scene

Drugs don't appear to be a major part of life at Stanford. The most popular substance that is used, and sometimes abused, is alcohol. The only drug that students mention with frequency is marijuana, which is probably more popular at Stanford than smoking cigarettes. Most Stanford students have never used or even witnessed others using anything harder than pot. Students are generally happy with the level of drug use (or, more appropriately, lack of drug use) on campus. Both the drinkers and pot smokers do their own thing and generally don't cause problems for others. If you're not into drugs, you won't be subject to any real social pressure to try them.

Most students at Stanford drink, and probably 20–25 percent of students smoke pot to some extent, ranging from isolated experimentation to near-daily usage. The use of harder drugs is very limited. That's not to say they're entirely absent from campus, but certainly nothing to be concerned with. At a school where academics outweigh nearly every other scene, you're not likely to find many students willing to compromise their studies for a quick fix of any kind.

The College Prowler® Grade on
Drug Scene: A-

A high grade in the Drug Scene indicates that drugs are not a noticeable part of campus life; drug use is not visible, and no pressure to use them seems to exist.

Campus Strictness

The Lowdown On...
Campus Strictness

What Are You Most Likely to Get Caught Doing on Campus?

- Biking without a headlight
- Biking through a stop sign
- Biking with an unregistered bike
- Biking drunk
- Carrying alcohol as a minor (Minor in Possession, or MIP)
- Parking illegally
- Sharing copyrighted music or movies outside the campus network

Students Speak Out On...
Campus Strictness

> "They're not strict at all. Just don't be dumb about what you're doing. Here, you can have alcohol in your room and drink it with the door open, and your RAs won't get mad or anything."

Q "I drink a fair amount and have never gotten in trouble for it. **Just be relatively well behaved, and don't make a fool of yourself** outside, and you should be cool. The same goes for drugs and such."

Q "It's best to be careful about whatever you're doing, not necessarily because you'll be caught, but because **nobody likes it when there's puke in the hallway**. It doesn't happen very often, but when it does, everyone gets pissed."

Q "**You can get away with most things**, but if you go overboard with something, your dormmates will probably at least be worried."

Q "**As long as you are in a dorm, anything goes**. The drinking policy is typically not enforced, as long as you aren't running around in the streets with stuff."

Q "This is one area in which Stanford does very well: **we get to have parties in our dorms with alcohol, and the police almost never come**. RAs are not policemen, and are cool with us drinking, as long as we are responsible about it."

Q "**Campus police are not that strict at all in my opinion**, in terms of drinking at least. About drugs, I'm not so sure. I know that last summer some students got expelled, but that's not something that happens very often."

Q "**We have these things here called MIPs**—Minor in Possession—and if you're caught doing something while drunk, and you're under 21, you get a ticket. But that's only if you're causing trouble or walking around outside with alcohol or something. You won't get busted if you're drinking in your room."

Q "Campus police are pretty laid-back. **Just don't walk down the street with a beer bottle, if you're underage**. You can totally drink in your dorm rooms and do pretty much whatever you want. It's much more laid-back than most schools here."

Q "The police only bother you in regards to traffic rules. **Students are basically treated like adults**."

Q "**Apparently, the police look the other way, with regards to underage drinking**, but they tend to tag you for stuff like riding an unlicensed bike, or a bike with no light."

Q "**I don't think there are campus rules**. Police don't ever break anything up—though they'll video tape some parties."

The College Prowler Take On...
Campus Strictness

Historically, Stanford has taken a laissez-faire approach toward alcohol. RAs and Resident Fellows (faculty members living next to dorms) are not expected to police rooms. Students are given a lot of freedom, with the hope that they will make responsible decisions. Police still have to enforce laws on campus, but they generally don't enter dorms. They mostly spend their time ticketing people for offenses like biking or driving through stop signs, and other assorted traffic violations. They generally don't interfere with parties, unless things get out of hand.

With that said, things seem to be changing. In recent years, the administration has taken a progressively tougher stance on alcohol, which has been banned in freshman dorms. Realistically, this means freshmen can no longer hold parties involving alcohol in common areas. RAs generally don't enforce this, but if the police were to show up, the consequences could be serious for both residents and staff. Stanford's original philosophy was to keep drinking out in the open so it could be moderated. Now they are trying to discourage it altogether. For the most part, freshmen can drink in their rooms, away from watchful RAs, but at frat or house parties, there are more strict carding policies—which are working, to an extent. The issue is very big on campus, and it's not clear what will happen. Chances are that the administration will continue to enforce stricter policies.

A-

The College Prowler® Grade on

Campus Strictness: A-

A high Campus Strictness grade implies an overall lenient atmosphere; police and RAs are fairly tolerant, and the administration's rules are flexible.

Parking

The Lowdown On...
Parking

Approximate Parking Permit Cost:
$130

Parking Services:
transportation@stanford.edu
(650) 723-9362
http://transportation.stanford.edu

Student Parking Lot?
Yes

Freshmen Allowed to Park?
No

Common Parking Tickets:

Expired Meter: $35

No Parking Zone: $35

Fire Lane: $50

Parking Permits:

Available to all undergrads except freshmen. Residents can purchase permits for the lot closest to their residence halls; commuters cannot get residence hall permits, but have a lot more choice in other campus lots.

Students Speak Out On...
Parking

"If you are a freshman, then no car for you! This is probably because finding parking on campus is already so tough."

Q "**You won't have to worry about parking** because freshmen aren't allowed to have cars."

Q "**Parking sucks**. You have to pay for a permit, and since a lot of people work here, it's difficult to find a parking spot during the day. By the dorms, it's okay, though. Whether parking will be difficult or not really depends on the dorm you live in."

Q "**Freshmen don't get cars**. You can get a parking permit starting your sophomore year. It's fairly easy to find a parking space on campus."

Q "There is a lot of parking, and from what I've heard about other schools, it's pretty cheap, too. You can't have a car as a freshman, but this makes you **focus more on campus life**. Later on in your college career, it might be nice to have a car, or at least to have friends with cars, so that you can get out every now and then."

Q "**There's a big parking problem here, which sucks**! It depends on where you live, though. There are definitely parking spaces if you get a student pass, but some dorms have many more spaces than others. So depending on where you live, you might find parking to be a hassle, or a breeze."

Q "Freshmen don't have cars, so **the rest of us can park**."

Q "Upperclassmen can bring cars to campus, and **there's plenty of parking** near where you live."

Q "Freshmen aren't allowed to have cars. Upperclassmen can always park, but **it is kind of a problem**."

Q "Freshmen can't have cars on campus, but there are ways around that. However, it makes parking pretty great for upperclassmen. **No complaints here**."

The College Prowler Take On...
Parking

Students are generally happy with the amount of available parking on campus. For a few years now, freshmen haven't been allowed to have cars or get permits, which has alleviated the parking problem. There are lots around campus where parking is still an issue, especially in large dorms that house all upperclassmen. In the worst case, you will have to park anywhere from a two to five minute walk away from your dorm during peak parking hours.

In general, having a car at Stanford will be fairly convenient. You can park right near your dorm during the day, and drive around and park at your friends' dorms across campus later at night. At $130 for a permit, it's pretty affordable. However, since incoming freshmen are not allowed to park on campus, you will have a whole year before parking will be a problem for you.

The College Prowler® Grade on
Parking: B

A high grade in this section indicates that parking is both available and affordable, and that parking enforcement isn't overly severe.

Transportation

The Lowdown On...
Transportation

Ways to Get Around Town:

On Campus
The Marguerite Shuttle runs around the perimeter of the Stanford campus, and it also travels out to the shopping mall, the medical park, and other popular areas. Most lines run from 6 a.m. to 8 p.m. during the week. Additional lines run 8 p.m.–12 a.m. all week, and as late as 2:30 a.m. on Friday and Saturday. It is free to Stanford students and the general public.

Public Transportation
Santa Clara Valley Transport Authority (VTA)
Buses serving the entire Silicon Valley area
http://www.vta.org

Bay Area Rapid Transit (BART)
Subways serving San Francisco, Berkeley, and the East Bay
http://www.bart.gov

CalTrain
Train service running along the peninsula from San Jose up to San Francisco
http://www.caltrain.org

➡

Taxi Cabs
Yellow Cab
(650) 324-1234

Yellow Cab AAA
(650) 361-1234

Airport Shuttles
South & East Bay
(800) 548-4664
SuperShuttle
(650) 246-8942

Car Rentals
Alamo, local: (650) 856-4147;
national: 1-800-327-9633,
www.alamo.com

Avis, local: (650) 493-8888;
national: 1-800-831-2847,
www.avis.com

Budget, local: (650) 424-0684;
national: 1-800-527-0700,
www.budget.com

Enterprise, local:
(650) 833-8060; national:
1-800-736-8222,
www.enterprise.com

Hertz, local: (650) 617-0386;
national: 1-800-654-3131,
www.hertz.com

National, local: (650) 856-9100;
national: 1-800-227-7368,
www.nationalcar.com

Best Ways to Get Around Town
Car
Bicycle
A friend with a car

Ways to Get Out of Town:

Airlines Serving San Francisco
American Airlines,
1-800-433-7300,
www.americanairlines.com

Continental, 1-800-523-3273,
www.continental.com

Delta, 1-800-221-1212,
www.delta.com

Northwest, 1-800-225-2525,
www.nwa.com

TWA, 1-800-221-2000,

United, 1-800-241-6522,
www.united.com

US Airways, 1-800-428-4322,
www.usairways.com

Additional Airlines Serving San Jose
Southwest, (800) 435-9792,
www.southwest.com

Airport
San Francisco Internal Airport
(650) 821-8211
The San Francisco International
Airport (SFO) is located
22 miles north of Stanford.

How to Get There
Drive north from Campus on
Route 101 and get off at the
SFO exit. Or take Route 280
north, then follow Route 380
over to the airport. It takes
30-60 minutes, depending
on traffic.

Via Public Transit

Take CalTrain from Palo Alto to Millbrae ($3), then take the free shuttle in Millbrae to the airport. It takes about an hour if you time it correctly.

Take a shuttle (South & East Bay is the cheapest) and be picked up and dropped off right at the airport. It takes about an hour, and costs $22.

Mineta San Jose Internal Airport

(408) 501-7600
San Jose International Airport (SJC) is located about seventeen miles south of Stanford.

How to Get There

Drive south from campus on Route 101 or 280, and take the exit for Route 87. Follow Route 87 to the airport. Takes 30-60 minutes, depending on traffic.

Via Public Transit

Take CalTrain from Palo Alto to Santa Clara ($3), then take the free shuttle to the airport. Takes about an hour if you time it correctly.

Take a shuttle and be picked up and dropped off right at the airport. (costs $25)

Greyhound

The Greyhound Trailways Bus Terminal is in Sunnyvale, approximately 13 miles from campus. For schedule information, call 1-800-231-2222 or visit *www.greyhound.com.*

Amtrak

The nearest station is located in Santa Clara at the Great America station, about fifteen miles south of Stanford. For schedule information, call 1-800-872-7245 or visit *www.amtrak.com.*

Santa Clara - Great America (GAC)

Foot Of Stars and Stripes Dr. Santa Clara, CA 95054

Travel Agents

Palo Alto Village Travel
105 Town & Country Village, Palo Alto
(650) 326-0510

Travel CUTS
Tresidder Memorial Union Floor 2, Stanford
(650) 470-0050

STA Travel
267 University Avenue, Palo Alto
(650) 322-4790

Students Speak Out On...
Transportation

> **"Public transportation is cool. Stanford has a free shuttle that takes you to the train station, shopping center, and to other places on campus. It's good."**

Q "**Everyone complains about our public transportation**, but it's as good as it gets in the Bay Area."

Q "We have **free shuttles that are relatively reliable**. The only problem is that there's no reason to go anywhere in the area around Stanford. Getting to the train station is pretty easy, though."

Q "Public transportation is very convenient. **It's easy to get to San Francisco**, or to anywhere around Palo Alto with the free campus shuttle."

Q "There is **a free shuttle that goes all around campus** that is pretty good. The CalTrain goes to San Francisco and San Jose, and makes many stops along the way."

Q "**The Marguerite is our free campus-shuttle**, but it takes a while, and doesn't go everywhere."

Q "Lately, it's been pretty fashionable to say bad things about our Marguerite Shuttle system, but I don't think it's that bad. I've also ridden the buses in Palo Alto a bit, and **those just require that you plan a little ahead**. CalTrain is reasonably priced, but not very fast. I found that it works well if you want to get to either airport; otherwise, you have to pay 20 bucks to take an airport shuttle. I've taken CalTrain to San Francisco a few times, and that's worked out pretty well."

Q "There's the Marguerite, which can take you around campus and the surrounding town, but that's not always reliable. **To get to the city you can ride the CalTrain**."

Q "**The Marguerite sucks, and it smells. Don't ever use it**. CalTrain is pretty convenient for getting to the city, and airports, and stuff. I never tried the buses on the peninsula, but SF has one of the better bus systems I've come across."

Q "The Marguerite definitely gets tiring after freshman year, although it is a very convenient way to get into Palo Alto and around campus your first year. **The CalTrain to San Francisco is expensive** at $9 to $10 round-trip, but sometimes you just have to get away. Hardly anyone knows the bus system, either, because they have a car or know someone who does, and that's that."

The College Prowler Take On...
Transportation

On campus, the only public transportation is the Marguerite Shuttle. Students don't find this service particularly useful, but a lot of carless freshmen use it to get downtown, or to the Stanford Shopping Center. Opinions on Bay Area transportation vary. Few students use the buses, but many take CalTrain to get to the airport or to San Francisco. In general, it will take at least an hour to get to the city and will cost about $9 roundtrip. San Francisco itself has great public transit, including MUNI buses and the BART subway system.

The Bay Area has a reasonably developed public transport system, but Stanford is a bit too isolated to take full advantage of it. You can take the Marguerite shuttle downtown, or to the mall, but you can't get to a standard grocery store. Ultimately, most Stanford students realize the necessity of having a car. You can get by without having one, but expect to spend a lot of time on campus.

The College Prowler® Grade on

Transportation: C-

A high grade for Transportation indicates that campus buses, public buses, cabs, and rental cars are readily-available and affordable. Other determining factors include proximity to an airport and the necessity of transportation.

Weather

The Lowdown On...
Weather

Average Temperature:

Fall:	72/50 °F
Winter:	60/42 °F
Spring:	71/49 °F
Summer:	78/56 °F

Average Precipitation:

Fall:	2.87 in.
Winter:	8.73 in.
Spring:	3.89 in.
Summer:	0.22 in.

Students Speak Out On...
Weather

{ **"We have very warm California weather. Bring light clothes, but remember to bring some more formal clothes for dances and other events."**

Q "The weather is probably one of the **most appealing attributes of this area**."

Q "**California's weather is nice**, especially when it is not too hot, but is still very sunny, and you get a nice breeze from the bay. It rains in the winter, but it doesn't get too cold."

Q "Typical bay-area weather is a little cooler than the weather in southern California. **It gets pretty cold at night here**."

Q "It's cold and rainy in the winter but **very beautiful at all other times**."

Q "**The weather here is amazing**. There is a rainy season, though, and it can get cold in the winter. Sometimes temperatures drop as low as 40 degrees."

Q "During the days, you can get away with very little clothing. The **evenings require something more substantial**."

Q "**This is Cali, so it is almost always nice**. However, unlike SoCal, we actually have more than one season."

Q "**It gets a bit nippy in the winter**, but is nothing compared to East Coast weather."

Q "There's **gorgeous weather here year-round**—mild, no humidity, sunny skies. It normally rains a lot in the winter, though."

The College Prowler Take On...
Weather

Students give Stanford overwhelmingly positive marks for weather. With the exception of winter, it is pretty much always sunny on campus, but still in the perfectly comfortable 60–75 degree range. Winters can be rainy, but it varies year to year. Summers can actually get pretty hot, but humidity is always reasonably low. It may get cold at night, but it's nothing compared to the weather in the Northeast. In general, the weather is great. The only time you will see snow is when your dorm takes a ski trip to Tahoe.

Maybe it's the weather, or maybe the prevailing California attitude, but be prepared to dress pretty light and informally throughout your time at Stanford. Expect to see shorts, T-shirts, and flip-flops for a large majority of the school year.

The College Prowler® Grade on

Weather: A-

A high Weather grade designates that temperatures are mild and rarely reach extremes, that the campus tends to be sunny rather than rainy, and that weather is fairly consistent rather than unpredictable.

Report Card Summary

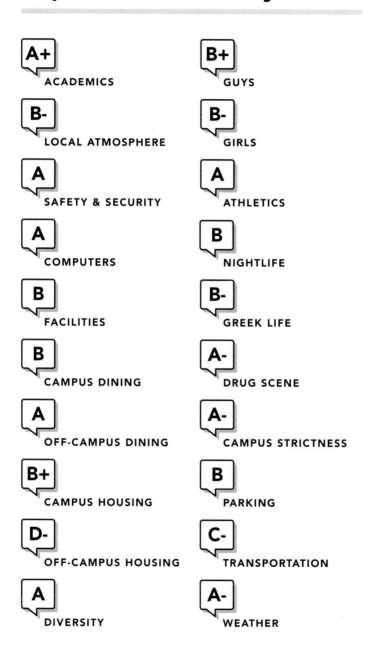

A+
ACADEMICS

B-
LOCAL ATMOSPHERE

A
SAFETY & SECURITY

A
COMPUTERS

B
FACILITIES

B
CAMPUS DINING

A
OFF-CAMPUS DINING

B+
CAMPUS HOUSING

D-
OFF-CAMPUS HOUSING

A
DIVERSITY

B+
GUYS

B-
GIRLS

A
ATHLETICS

B
NIGHTLIFE

B-
GREEK LIFE

A-
DRUG SCENE

A-
CAMPUS STRICTNESS

B
PARKING

C-
TRANSPORTATION

A-
WEATHER

Overall Experience

Students Speak Out On...
Overall Experience

{ **"This is the best school that I could have chosen for myself. I would recommend it over any other place!"**

Q **"The strength of this school is the people—the faculty and the students.** The vast majority of them are nothing short of amazing. While there are definitely things that I miss about being home, I like almost everything about being here."

Q "I don't know what it's like to attend school anywhere else, **but Stanford is an interesting, comfortable, and non-intimidating place to be.**"

Q "Stanford is an amazing place offering a great education, a great social life, and great sports. Palo Alto is a little dull, but San Francisco is nearby, and there are always a lot of things happening on campus. **I am incredibly happy here, and I think that it is the greatest place on earth**. It isn't for everyone, though."

Q "This is definitely the best place that I could be. It is academically rigorous, sometimes to the point of being painful, but there are also a lot of opportunities to have fun. It's up to you. I have made good faculty contacts, and anyone with a little initiative can find a way to work in a lab, or do some sort of independent project. **It's up to you to make sure that you get your money's worth**, but it's definitely possible."

Q "It's much **better than expected**."

Q "I honestly can't imagine being anywhere else, but I think everyone says that about his or her school. **I genuinely love Stanford**, though, because it is an awe-inspiring institution, while managing to be quirky and personal. I wouldn't trade my experiences here for anything."

Q "Stanford gives you great opportunities. The downside to attending Stanford is that it can feel competitive at times, and you might feel intimidated by that. The big thing to keep in mind is that many people are so smart and study so hard that they tend to be a little weird. But I have some great friends that are very down-to-earth. I am kind of bummed about the dating scene right now because I had a few girlfriends in high school, and now that's not the case. But **I am here mainly to learn**, so I am happy."

Q "This place is called 'Camp Stanford' for a reason. Palm trees, sun, a friendly and down-to-earth student body, and a flexible academic schedule are pretty much the makings of a design-your-own paradise. **People here care about succeeding**, but they care equally about friendship and savoring the time they have here. Consider it a challenging, rigorous, delightful vacation."

Q "**I have enjoyed my time at Stanford**. I have made many good friends, and I can honestly say that I have had a good education. The training I have received in my science and engineering classes has improved my reasoning abilities. Now, I feel as if I can tackle more difficult and complex problems."

Q "There is a misconception about Stanford that I would like to correct. **Everything you have heard about Stanford being a laid-back school is false**. The students may seem laid-back, but most of them are putting up a facade. A lot of people enter Stanford believing they will 'take it easy' and not worry so much about school and grades. But most of the people who say that soon realize that for their whole lives, their existence has centered around achievement and school. To suddenly change is unrealistic, to say the least. Almost everyone ends up studying a lot, and devoting most of their time to achieving whatever career goals they have in mind. This is not necessarily a bad thing; however, the sooner one realizes this prevailing attitude, the better off they'll be."

The College Prowler Take On...
Overall Experience

The verdict is in: most students are overwhelmingly happy with the Stanford experience. The combination of challenging academics, undergrad-oriented faculty, diverse students, beautiful weather, and a fairly social campus environment all combine to make for a great four years of college. Students, particularly those in engineering or sciences, might find the workload to be especially heavy at times, but most are capable and want to work hard in the first place. Perhaps the biggest challenge students face at Stanford is just dealing with the other students, who range from hippies to hyper-competitive pre-meds. It makes for an interesting environment, but also a stressful one. However, if you immerse yourself in it long enough, it will eventually start to feel reasonably normal.

Despite the problems that Stanford students find with the University, they overwhelmingly agree that Stanford is "their place," and can't imagine being anywhere else. It seems all the hype and the hefty price tag are well justified by the experiences that students can, and will, have here. If you're looking for a university with a big name, vibrant population, and a good balance of work and fun, Stanford University will not disappoint.

The Inside Scoop

The Lowdown On...
The Inside Scoop

Stanford Slang

Know the slang, know the school. The following is a list of words you really need to know before coming to Stanford. The more you know, the better off you'll be.

Chappie – The *Stanford Chaparral*, Stanford's nationally recognized, award-winning humor magazine

CS – Computer Science

CSRE – Not to be confused with CS, it stands for Comparative Studies in Race and Ethnicity

***Daily* Dawg** – Someone who works on the *Daily*, Stanford's weekly newspaper

Dormcest – Hooking up with someone in your own dorm

The Draw – The lottery process that assigns you to housing after freshman year

"Dropping the S-Bomb" – Saying the word "Stanford"; in order to get jobs or internships

Flicks – Every Sunday, movies are played in MemAud

FloMo – Florence Moore Hall

FroSoCo – Freshman/ Sophomore College

HumBio – Human Biology

IHUM – Introduction to the Humanities—a required sequence for freshmen

JRo – Junipero freshmen dorm

LSJUMB – Leland Stanford Junior University Marching Band—You'll love them freshman year, but after that you'll get sick of their antics.

MemAud – Memorial Auditorium

MemChu – Memorial Church

The Oval – The grassy strip in front of the Quad

ProFro – Prospective Freshman, in particular the ones who visit during Admit Weekend in April

Progressive – A dorm party where each room hosts a different mixed drink

PWR (Power) – Program in Writing and Rhetoric—also required for freshmen

The Quad – The red stone plaza where most classes are held

SLE – Structured Liberal Education—an-all year residential/academic option for freshmen

Su.market – An online newsgroup for buying and selling just about anything

TresEx – Tresidder Express, an overpriced convenience store in Tresidder

Things I Wish I Knew Before Coming to Stanford

• Friends don't always make the best roommates.

• Most people here are Type A personalities. And yet, Stanford students are almost never punctual.

• You can buy your textbooks much cheaper online.

• You will skip 9 a.m. classes.

• You won't eat more than 14 meals a week in the dining hall, usually even fewer.

• Prerequisites for classes are not enforced; take whatever you want, if you can handle the work.

• For most classes, you can collaborate with others on problem sets and assignments.

Tips to Succeed at Stanford

- Pick classes you actually like.
- Research your professors before choosing your classes.
- Actually go to class.
- Find a good study group.
- Go to office hours.
- If you study engineering, don't live in Manzanita. You will be depressed.
- Get out and go to parties.
- Join a student group, but don't join too many.

Stanford Urban Legends

CS Professor Eric Roberts was responsible for failing Bill Gates out of Harvard.

Stanford was started by Leland and Jane Stanford after they attempted to donate money to Harvard but were treated rudely because of their dirty clothes.

Thousands of dead horses are buried under the Quad from when Stanford was a Stock Farm.

School Spirit

Your average Stanford student is a walking advertisement for the University. Sit next to one on an airplane, and within half an hour she'll be talking your ear off about all the great things she's had the opportunity to do here. Sports are another apparent cause for school spirit, and most students will claim some interest in Cardinal athletics. When many of the teams are ranked number one, and your school has won numerous Sears Cups, it's an easy thing to take pride in. But practically speaking, most students don't really pay attention to sports, beyond reading the headlines in the *Daily*. Expect a bit of cynicism around midterms and finals, but otherwise students are overwhelmingly excited about the University.

Traditions

Full Moon on the Quad

On the night of the first full moon in fall quarter, tradition has it that freshman females and senior males come out onto the Quad and kiss at midnight. Over the years, the tradition has degenerated into all freshman and seniors making out, often under the influence of alcohol. Residents from the co-ops usually come and streak the event. Sophomores, juniors, and even grad-students may show up, too. The administration is trying to do away with this tradition.

Big Game

During fall quarter, toward the end of the football season, Stanford and Berkeley play each other in the annual Big Game. Each year, the venue alternates between the two campuses. The week leading up to the event is filled with rallies and pranks. The winner of Big Game gets to keep the highly coveted Ax for the following year. At one point, Stanford had held the Ax for seven seasons in a row, but finally had to give it up after a particularly pathetic loss to Cal.

Su.market

Su.market is a newsgroup that anyone on campus can access using a standard newsreader. Students, faculty, and staff post items for sale or items they want to buy. It includes everything from concert tickets to textbooks to cars. Check it out for some great deals.

Finding a Job or Internship

The Lowdown On...
Finding a Job or Internship

This is Stanford, so getting the perfect summer internship or great job is on everyone's mind. Stanford has great industry connections, and a Career Development Center to help students with the process. The CDC will help you write or revise your resume, provide you with literature about how to get a job, and give you access to a database of past and current opportunities.

Advice

Check out the CDC, and get there early—the first quarter of your freshman year is a great time to start. Once you've gotten into the system and figured out how everything works, it'll be a lot easier to take advantage of all the services CDC offers. Unlike some other schools, Career Services can be a busy place at Stanford; there are a lot of motivated students looking for jobs and internships, so it's important to make a name for yourself early on.

Career Center Resources & Services

Career Development Center
http://www.stanford.edu/dept/CDC

Stanford eProNet
http://stanford.epronet.com

Stanford Career Network
http://www.stanfordalumni.org/career

Cardinal Recruiting
http://cardinalcareers.stanford.edu

Grads Who Enter the Job Market Within 6 months:
55%

Firms That Most Frequently Hire Graduates:
Goldman Sachs, Microsoft, Oracle, Google, Bain

Alumni

The Lowdown On...
Alumni

Web site:
http://www.stanfordalumni.org

Office:
Frances C. Arrillaga
Alumni Center
326 Galvez Street
Stanford, CA 94305
(650) 724-0888

Services Available
Lifetime e-mail address
@stanfordalumni.org

Lifetime subscription to
Stanford Magazine

➜

Major Alumni Events

Every October, Stanford has Homecoming weekend. There is a football game, class reunions, and even a series of lectures for alumni. There are many other events throughout the year, all over the country. See the alumni events Web site for more information – *http://www.stanfordalumni.org/erc*

Alumni Publications

Stanford Magazine comes out six times a year and distributes to all current students, undergrad parents, and a vast network of alumni. Subscriptions are $24 per year.

Did You Know?

Famous Stanford Alums:

Steve Ballmer – CEO Microsoft

Sergey Brin and Lawrence Page – Founders of Google

Sandra Day O'Connor – Supreme Court Justice

John Elway – NFL quarterback

Carleton Fiorina – CEO Hewlett Packard

Herbert Hoover – President of the United States

Ted Koppel – *Nightline* anchor

Sally Ride – Astronaut

Sigourney Weaver – Actress

Tiger Woods – Professional golfer

Chih-Yuan "Jerry" Yang and David Filo – Founders of Yahoo!

Student Organizations

Stanford actually has over 600 registered student groups, in activities ranging from academics to sports to community service. For more information on any of these groups, visit *http://osa.stanford.edu/studentgroups*.

Academic

American Advertising Federation • American Indian Science and Engineering Society • Association for Radiological Sciences Students • Association of Women Academics in the Humanities and Social Sciences • BioMedically-Affiliated Stanford Students • Cap and Gown • Cashflow Group • ChinaRains • College Student Interest Group in Neurology • Engineers for a Sustainable World • Futurist Club • Gamma Zeta Alpha Fraternity • GSB Energy Club • GSB Real Estate Club • GSB Sports Management Club • GSB Telecom Club • Hopkins Marine Station Undergraduate Club • JD/MBA Association • Mechanical Engineering Graduate Women's Group • Online Course Guide • Performance Automotive Engineering Club • Product Design Student Association • Society for Industrial and Applied Mathematics • Society of Black Scientists and Engineers •

Society of Petroleum Engineers • Society of Women Engineers • Sophomore Class Presidents (2006) • Alpine Project • Astrobiology Association • Astronomical Society • BioLaw • Debate Society • Economics Association • Engineering Association • INFORMS • International Human Rights Law Association • Journal of International Relations • Journal of Law, Business, & Finance • Law Review • Medical Students Association • Mock Trial • Political Science Association • Psi Chi • Solar Car Project • Student Biodesign • Undergraduate Psychology Association • Stanford University Mathematical Organization • Yan Xin Life Science Technology Association • Student Initiated Courses • SUSE Student Guild • Tau Beta Pi • Women in Computer Science

Athletic

Aiki-Weapons • Cardinal Competitive Cheer • Cardinal Whirlwinds • Graduate Rugby Club • GSB Soccer Club • GSB Ultimate Frisbee Club • Hwa Rang Kwan Tae Kwon Do & Hapkido • JKA Shotokan of Stanford • Jujitsu Club • Men's Ultimate • Orienteering Club • Quiz Bowl Club • Ski & Snowboard Club • Aerobics and Yoga • Aikido Club • Alpine Club • Alpine Ski Team • Archery Program • AXE Committee • Badminton Club • Beach Volleyball Club • Canoe and Kayak Team • Capoeira • Climbing Wall Club • Club Ice Hockey • Club Sports • Club Triathlon Team • Contract Bridge Club • Cricket Club • Cycling • Dressage Club • Equestrian Team • Figure Skating Club • Gaming Society • Graduate School of Business Golf Club • Judo Club Team • Kayak Club • Kenpo Karate Association • Kokondo Academy • Martial Arts Program • Men's Club Soccer Team • Men's Lacrosse • Muay Thai • Polo Club • Rugby Football Club • Running Club • Shorin-Ryu Karate • Shotokan • Squash Men's Intercollegiate Team • Squash Women's Intercollegiate Team • Table Tennis Club • Taekwondo • Tennis Club • Wing Chun Student Association • Waterski Team • Women's Club Soccer • Women's Rugby • Women's Ultimate • Wushu Club • Universal Karate Club •

The Nomadic Shoe Store • Triathlon Running Club • Wave Riders • Women's Club Lacrosse Team

Community Service

49ers Academy Teaching Team • Alpha Kappa Alpha Sorority • Alpha Phi Alpha • Alpha Phi Omega • Alternative Spring Break • American Red Cross • Amnesty International • Arbor Free Clinic Literacy Project • Artspan • Asian American Initiative for Youth Motivation and Empowerment • Barrio Assistance • Best Buddies • Board Fellows • Campus Girl Scouts • Challenge 4 Charity • Circle K • Delta Sigma Theta • Dosti • East Palo Alto Stanford Academy • East Palo Alto Tennis and Tutoring • Educational Democracy for Youth • Educational Studies Program • Future Alumni Consulting Team • GSB Gives Back • Habla La Noche • Health Education—Lifetime Partnerships for Kids • Henry's Place • I Have a Dream • Kids With Dreams • Los Hermanos de Stanford • March of Dimes Collegiate Council • Mensola • Native American Tutoring Project • Night Outreach • Organ Donor Education • Pacific Free Clinic • PALS • Perspectives into Career Opportunities • Pilipino American Student Union • Project Motivation • SAT Success • Science and Environmental Education • Side by Side • Alliance for Service through the Arts • Amateur Radio Club • Anthology for Youth • Bike Advocates • Community Carnival • Community Farm • ESL Partners • Habitat for Humanity • Health Corps • Project on Hunger • StreetLaw • Minority Medical Alliance • Upward Bound • V-day • Youth Forensics • Youth Project • Start Up • Student Committee For Community Lawyering • Students Who Love SPILF • Technology Assist By Students • The Giving Tree • The Science Bus • Together Each Achieves More • Tzu Chi Collegiate Association • United Students for Veterans' Health • Women and Youth Supporting Each Other

Creative Arts

Alliance Streetdance • Asian American Theater Project • Audio Engineering Society • Beat Junkies • Bent Spoon Dance Company • Blackstage • Cardinal Ballet Company • Counterpoint a cappella • Decadance • Double or Nothing Swing Dance Ensemble • Down With Gravity • DV8 • Everyday People • GSB Show • Hindi Film Dance Team • Hip Hop Congress • Innovative Student Information Services • Israeli Folk Dancing @ Stanford • Jam Pac'd • Kayumanggi • Knitting Renaissance • Kuumba African Dance Ensemble • Leland Stanford Junior University Marching Band • Los Salseros de Stanford • Mariachi Cardenal de Stanford • Mixed Company • Noopur • Raas-Garba (Indian Folk) Competitive Dance Team • Ram's Head Theatrical Society • Ballroom Dance Club • Ballroom Dance Team • Bhangra Team • Chamber Chorale • Concert Network • Cooking Club • Film Society • Fleet Street Singers • Gospel Choir • Harmonics • Hwimori • Improvisors • Jazz Orchestra • Law School Drama Society • Mendicants • Opera Society • Raagapella • Savoyards • Shakespeare Society • Spoken Word Collective • Steppers • Swing Kids • Symphony Orchestra • Taiko • Tango Club • University Singers • Wind Ensemble • Step Out • Student Organizing Committee for the Arts • Swingtime • Talisman • Tapdance@Stanford • Testimony A Cappella • Tomboys: Stanford's Humorous Music Interpreters • Urban Styles • Viennese Ball Committee

Ethnic/Cultural

African American Fraternal and Sororal Association • Aguila Real A.C. • Akwaaba, Ghanaian Students' Association • Alaska Native Sudent Association • Argentinos en Stanford • Armenian Students Association • Asian American Graduate Students Association • Asian American Student Association • Asian Pacific American Medical Student • Asian Pacific Islander Law Students Association •

Asian/Pacific Islander Heritage Month • Association of Chinese Students and Scholars at Stanford • Ballet Folklorico de Stanford • BELGICA • Black and Queer at Stanford • Black Business Student Association • Black Family Gathering Committee • Black Graduate Students Association • Black Graduation Committee • Black Law Students Association • Black Liberation Month Planning Committee • Black Recruitment Orientation Committee • Black Student Union • Brazilian Students Association • Caribbean Students Association • Central American Student Association at Stanford • Cherokee Student Group • Chicano Latino Graduate Student Association • Community of Stanford Students with Disabilities • Cornerstone • Creation Outreach Respect and Education • Cultural Interaction Club • Dine Club • Estonian Student Association at Stanford • European Association at Stanford • French Stanford Student Association • Graduate School of Business South Asian Association • Graduate Women's Network • GSB Europe Club • GSB Texas Club • Hellenic Association of Stanford • Hispanic Business Students Association • Hong Kong Student Association • Hopkins Marine Station Graduate Student Organization • Hui o Hawai'i • Iberia - Spanish Association at Stanford • Indonesian Club at Stanford • Inphanyte Records, aka SURGE • Intercollegiate Taiwanese American Students Association • International Undergraduate Community • Israeli Student Organization • Kennedy Kosher Coop • Korean Student Association at Stanford • Korean-American Student Association • Lambda Theta Nu • Latino 06 Council • Latino Medical Student Association • Lebanese Student Association at Stanford • Malaysians at Stanford University • Mexican Student Association • Multiracial Identified Community at Stanford • Muslim Students Awareness Network • Muwekma Residents • Native American Law Students Association • Nepali Association at Stanford • Nigerian Students Association (Naija) • Organization of Arab-American Students In Stanford • Pakistanis at Stanford • Persian Student Association • Peruanos en Stanford • Q-BEC, Siociete des Harfangs Perdus •

Queer and Questioning Asians And Pacific Islanders • Romanian Student Association • Saheli • Sanskriti • Satrang, Stanford Sikh Students Association • Scandinavians at Stanford • Sigma Theta Psi • Singaporeans at Stanford • Sisters At Stanford • Sri Lankan Student Association • African Students Association • American Indian Gays • American Indian Organization • American Indigenous Medical Students • Asian Kitchen Club • Australia Club • Cambodian Cultural Association • Egyptian Association • Ethiopian Student Union • German Student Association • Graduate School of Business Asian Society • GSB Asian Society • GSB Canadian Club • Hawaii Club • India Association • Japan Exchange Club • Jewish Medical Student Association • Latino Law Students Association • Native American Graduate Students • Newtype • Powwow • Queer Engineers and Scientists • Serbian Student Society • Taiwanese Student Association • University Nikkei • Taiwanese Cultural Society • THai-American Intercultural Society • The Chicano/Latino Big Sib/Lil Sib Program • Turkish Student Association • Ukrainian Student Association at Stanford • Undergraduate Chinese American Association • UNIDAS • Venezuelan Association at Stanford • Vietnamese Student Association

Health and Wellness

American Medical Students Association • Arbor Free Clinic • Chicanos Latinos in Health Education • Colleges Against Cancer • MIRROR • Nepal Clinical Internship • Organization of International Health • Peer Anonymous HIV Test Counselors • Sexual Health Peer Resources Center • South Asian Preventive Health Outreach Program • Environmental Health Interest Group • Yoga Club • Student Interest Group in Psychiatry • studentErgonomics.org • The Bridge Peer Counseling Center • The Green Team • Women's Health Interest Group

Media/Publications

Branner Presents • Enigma Magazine • Expression! • Inner Peace Forum • KZSU 90.1 FM • Lit Magazine • Masque Magazine • Reorient Magazine • Six Degrees • Soul Sistah Magazine • Cardinal Broadcasting Network Television • Stanford Chaparral • Journal of Civil Rights and Civil Liberties • Journal of East Asian Affairs • News Readership Program • Scientific Review • Technology Law Review • Undergraduate Research Journal • The Mind's Eye • The Real News • The Daily • The Progressive • The Quad • The Review • Vagabond • Womenspeak • Word Choice • The Dualist • Rational Thought

Political/Social Awareness

American Constitution Society • Asha for Education • Speakers Bureau • Bursting the Bubble: Discuss Current Events • Coalition For Justice • Effective Environmental Solutions at Stanford • Environmental Law Society • Federalist Society • Feminist Collective • Forum For American/Chinese Exchange At Stanford • Greens at Stanford • GSB Government & Politics Club • La Familia de Stanford • LGBT-Meds • Medical Students for Choice • Movimiento Estudiantil Chicano de Aztlan • Out4Biz: The LGBT-Straight Alliance for • Physicians for Human Rights • Physicians for Social Responsibility • Querillas • Redwood Action Team at Stanford • Shaking the Foundations Conference • Society for International Affairs at Stanford • Air Force Club • Asian American Activism Coalition • Association for International Development • Campaign for Equal Justice • College Republicans • Community for Peace and Justice • Conservative Union • Democrats • Emergency Medical Services • Stanford In Government • Israel Alliance • Jewish American Alliance • Labor Action Coalition • Law School Democrats • Malaysia Forum • National Association for the Advancement of Colored People • Students For Choice • Students for Clark • Students for Howard Dean • Students for Life • Vegan Action • Student Campaign for Child Survival •

Student Global AIDS Campaign • Students for a Sustainable
Stanford • Students for Environmental Justice At Stanford

Pre-Professional

Alpha Kappa Psi • American Society of Civil Engineers •
American Society of Mechanical Engineers • Army ROTC • Asia
Technology Initiative • Asia-Pacific Student Entreprenuership
Society • Black Pre Business Society • Black Pre-Law Society
• Business Association of Stanford Engineering Students •
California Medical Association/American Medical Association
• Derechos • Emergency Medicine Interest Group • Family
Medicine Interest Group • Future Social Innovators Network •
Graduate School of Business Off Duty Club • GSB Arts, Media
& Entertainment Club • GSB Entrepreneurship Club • GSB
Environmental Management Club • GSB Finance & Investment
Club • GSB Greater China Business Club • GSB High Tech Club
• GSB Marketing Club • GSB Product Design and Manufacturing
Club • GSB Retail Club • GSB Social Venture Club • GSB Travel
& Hospitality Club • GSB Venture Capital Club • Health Care
and Biotech Club • Kappa Alpha Psi Fraternity Incorporated
• Obstetrics and Gynecology Interest Group • Partnership for
Education • Political Science Graduate Students Association
• Redefining Our Premed Experience at Stanford • Alumni
Mentoring • Black Pre-Medical Organization • Consulting
• Engineered Solutions • Graduate School of Business •
Management Consulting Club • GSB Healthcare & Biotechnology
Club • GSB Private Equity & Buyouts Club • Institute of Electrical
and Electronics Engineers • Law & Technology Association • Law
& Wine Society • Law School Mock Trial Team • Management
Internship Fund • Pre-Business Association • Pre-Law Society •
Premedical Association • Society Of Chicano/Latino Engineers
and Scientists • Undergraduate Minority Business Association
• University Macintosh User Group • Student National
Medical Association • The Charles R. Blyth Fund • TiE YE •

Wilderness Medicine Interest Group • Women in Management • Women Leaders of Tomorrow

Recreational

GSB Outdoor Adventures • Israeli Folk Dancing at Stanford • Jewish Leadership Council • Korean Christian Fellowship • Chess Club • Croquet Club • Windsurfing and Kiteboarding Club • Asian Baptist Student Koinonia • Bahai Association at Stanford • Buddhist Community at Stanford • Cardinal Life • Catholic Community at Stanford • Chabad at Stanford • Chi Alpha Christian Fellowship • Chinese Campus Evangelistic Fellowship • Chinese Christian Fellowship at Stanford • Christian Science Organization • Elijah Christian Cell Group at Stanford • Episcopal - Lutheran Campus Ministry • Fellowship in Christ at Stanford • Graduate School of Business Christian Fellowship • Great Commission Movement • GSB Jewish Business Students Assoc. • Harvest Christian Fellowship • International Students Christian Outreach • Intervarsity Christian Fellowship • InterVarsity Graduate Christian Fellowship • Islamic Society • Jewish Law Students Association • Jewish Women's Collective • Latter-day Saint Student Association • Lutheran Student Fellowship at Stanford • Orthodox Christian Fellowship • Parakaleo Christian Ministries • Questus: GSB Catholic Community • Reformed University Fellowship at Stanford • ReJoyce in Jesus Campus Fellowship • Sports Challenge • Young Life Leader Association • Students for The truth • Unitarian Universalists at Stanford • World Peace Buddhists • Zoroastrians At Stanford

Social

Advanced Degree Student Organization of Stanford Law School • Alpha Delta Phi Literary Society • Alpha Epsilon Pi • Alpha Kappa Delta Phi • Chi Omega • Chicano/Latino Graduation • Class of 2004 • Class of 2005 • Class of 2007 ASSU-Freshman Council • Delta Delta Delta • Delta Kappa Epsilon • Delta Tau Delta • Epicureans at the GSB • Graduate School Of Business Africa Business Club • Graduate School of Business PhD Association • GSB Card Club • GSB Dogs • GSB Latin American Student Association • GSB Orientation • GSB Yearbook • Inter-Fraternity Council • Inter-Sorority Council • Jewish Student Association • Kappa Alpha • Kappa Alpha Theta • Kappa Kappa Gamma • Kappa Sigma • Lambda Phi Epsilon • Michigan Club of Stanford • Phi Kappa Psi Fraternity • Pi Beta Phi • Redwood Outdoor Club • Sigma Alpha Epsilon • Sigma Chi • Sigma Nu • Sigma Phi Epsilon • Sigma Psi Zeta • Business School Students' Association • GSB Wine Circle • Japanese Association • Outing Club • Yanyuan Club

The Best & Worst

The Ten **BEST** Things About Stanford:

1. The weather
2. Beautiful campus
3. San Francisco
4. Talented, compassionate professors
5. Great parties
6. Diversity
7. On-campus housing
8. Getting a job
9. Wireless Internet
10. Great athletics

The Ten **WORST** Things About Stanford:

1 An increasingly stringent administration

2 Palo Alto

3 Egomaniacs

4 Cost of living and tuition

5 The Student Union

6 All-nighters

7 PWR

8 Expensive photocopies and printing

9 Dorm food (after 20 weeks)

10 Finishing spring quarter halfway through June

Visiting

The Lowdown On...
Visiting

Hotel Information:

Stanford-Operated

SLAC Guest House
2575 Sand Hill Road,
Menlo Park
(650) 926-2800
*http://www.stanford.edu/dept/
hds/SLAC*
Price Range: $50-$120
Distance from Campus:
2.2 miles

Palo Alto

The Cardinal Hotel
235 Hamilton Avenue, 94301
(650) 323-5101
http://www.cardinalhotel.com
Price Range: $76-$120
Distance from Campus:
1 Miles

Coronet Motel
2455 El Camino, 94306
(650) 326-1081
Price Range: $50-$75
Distance from Campus:
1.7 miles

Garden Court Hotel

520 Cowper Street, 94301

(650) 322-9000

http://www.gardencourt.com

Price Range: $170+

Distance from Campus:
1.4 miles

Hotel California

2431 Ash Street, 94306

(650) 322-7666

http://www.hotelcalifornia.com

Price Range: $76-$120

Distance from Campus:
1.7 miles

Sheraton Palo Alto Hotel

625 El Camino, 94301

(650) 328-2800

http://www.sheraton.com

Price Range: $170+

Distance from Campus:
0.8 miles

Stanford Terrace Inn

531 Stanford Avenue, 94306

(650) 857-0333

*http://www.stanfordterraceinn.
com*

Price Range: $121-170

Distance from Campus:
1.2 miles

Super 8 Motel

3200 El Camino, 94306

(650) 493-9085

http://www.super8paloalto.com

Price Range: $76-$120

Distance from Campus:
2.1 miles

Travelodge

3255 El Camino, 94306

(650) 493-6340

http://www.travelodge.com

Price Range: $76-$175

Distance from Campus:
2.1 miles

Menlo Park

Best Western Riviera

15 El Camino, 94025

(650) 321-8772

http://www.bestwestern.com

Price Range: $121-170

Distance from Campus:
1.4 miles

Stanford Park Hotel

100 El Camino, 94025

(650) 322-1234

*http://www.stanfordparkhotel
.com*

Price Range: $170+

Distance from Campus:
1.4 miles

Take a Campus Virtual Tour

Although Stanford presently doesn't advertise a virtual tour, they do have a video of campus, which requires RealPlayer, online at *http://admission.stanford.edu/visiting*.

Campus Tours

Free tours are available twice a day, seven days a week. Tours depart from Vistor Information Services, in Memorial Auditorium, at 11 a.m. and 3:15 p.m. Tours are offered year-round, except during the winter holiday break and certain holidays. For more information, call (650) 723-2560 or e-mail visitorinfo@stanford.edu.

To Schedule a Group Information Session

Call the Office of Undergraduate Admission to make a reservation, at (650) 725-5294. Stanford does not do interviews of any sort for undergraduate admission.

Overnight Visits

Stanford does not provide overnight visits for prospective applicants, except in the case of athletic or diversity recruitment. However, if you are admitted to Stanford, you can, and should, come to Admit Weekend in mid-April. About 800 prospective freshmen (ProFros) come to Admit Weekend to check out Stanford and stay in the dorms from Thursday to Sunday. Keep in mind, this is Stanford's way to convince you to come to the school, and most people will be trying hard to make the place look good. Still, you can get a reasonably accurate impression of the place and get a good sense of what the people are like. Admit Weekend is completely dry.

Directions to Campus

From Highway 101 (North or South)

- Take the Embarcadero Road exit west toward Stanford.
- At El Camino Real, Embarcadero turns into Galvez Street; stay in the left lane and head toward the center of campus.
- Metered parking is available on the streets.
- The Visitor Information Center is located in Memorial Hall, on Serra Street across from Hoover Tower.

From Highway 280 (North or South)

- Take the Sand Hill Road east, turning right at the traffic light on Santa Cruz Avenue.
- Make an immediate left onto Junipero Serra Boulevard.
- Turn at Campus Drive East, which is the second stoplight.
- Turn left when you reach Serra Street (there's a gas station), and follow Serra Street until it ends.
- Turn right onto Galvez, and there will be parking adjacent to Memorial Hall.

From El Camino Real

- Take the University Avenue exit, and turn away from Palo Alto.
- University Avenue will become Palm Drive as you enter Stanford.
- Make a left after the first traffic light, onto Campus Drive.
- Then turn right onto Galvez Street at the next stop sign.
- There will be parking adjacent to Memorial Hall.

Words to Know

Academic Probation – A suspension imposed on a student if he or she fails to keep up with the school's minimum academic requirements. Those unable to improve their grades after receiving this warning can face dismissal.

Beer Pong / Beirut – A drinking game involving cups of beer arranged in a pyramid shape on each side of a table. The goal is to get a ping pong ball into one of the opponent's cups by throwing the ball or hitting it with a paddle. If the ball lands in a cup, the opponent is required to drink the beer.

Bid – An invitation from a fraternity or sorority to 'pledge' (join) that specific house.

Blue-Light Phone – Brightly-colored phone posts with a blue light bulb on top. These phones exist for security purposes and are located at various outside locations around most campuses. In an emergency, a student can pick up one of these phones (free of charge) to connect with campus police or a security escort.

Campus Police – Police who are specifically assigned to a given institution. Campus police are typically not regular city officers; they are employed by the university in a full-time capacity.

Club Sports – A level of sports that falls somewhere between varsity and intramural. If a student is unable to commit to a varsity team but has a lot of passion for athletics, a club sport could be a better, less intense option. Even less demanding, intramural (IM) sports often involve no traveling and considerably less time.

Cocaine – An illegal drug. Also known as "coke" or "blow," cocaine often resembles a white crystalline or powdery substance. It is highly addictive and dangerous.

Common Application – An application with which students can apply to multiple schools.

Course Registration – The period of official class selection for the upcoming quarter or semester. Prior to registration, it is best to prepare several back-up courses in case a particular class becomes full. If a course is full, students can place themselves on the waitlist, although this still does not guarantee entry.

Division Athletics – Athletic classifications range from Division I to Division III. Division IA is the most competitive, while Division III is considered to be the least competitive.

Dorm – A dorm (or dormitory) is an on-campus housing facility. Dorms can provide a range of options from suite-style rooms to more communal options that include shared bathrooms. Most first-year students live in dorms. Some upperclassmen who wish to stay on campus also choose this option.

Early Action – An application option with which a student can apply to a school and receive an early acceptance response without a binding commitment. This system is becoming less and less available.

Early Decision – An application option that students should use only if they are certain they plan to attend the school in question. If a student applies using the early decision option and is admitted, he or she is required and bound to attend that university. Admission rates are usually higher among students who apply through early decision, as the student is clearly indicating that the school is his or her first choice.

Ecstasy – An illegal drug. Also known as "E" or "X," ecstasy looks like a pill and most resembles an aspirin. Considered a party drug, ecstasy is very dangerous and can be deadly.

Ethernet – An extremely fast Internet connection available in most university-owned residence halls. To use an Ethernet connection properly, a student will need a network card and cable for his or her computer.

Fake ID – A counterfeit identification card that contains false information. Most commonly, students get fake IDs with altered birthdates so that they appear to be older than 21 (and therefore of legal drinking age). Even though it is illegal, many college students have fake IDs in hopes of purchasing alcohol or getting into bars.

Frosh – Slang for "freshman" or "freshmen."

Hazing – Initiation rituals administered by some fraternities or sororities as part of the pledging process. Many universities have outlawed hazing due to its degrading and sometimes dangerous nature.

Intramurals (IMs) – A popular, and usually free, sport league in which students create teams and compete against one another. These sports vary in competitiveness and can include a range of activities—everything from billiards to water polo. IM sports are a great way to meet people with similar interests.

Keg – Officially called a half-barrel, a keg contains roughly 200 12-ounce servings of beer.

LSD – An illegal drug. Also known as acid, this hallucinogenic drug most commonly resembles a tab of paper.

Marijuana – An illegal drug. Also known as weed or pot; along with alcohol, marijuana is one of the most commonly-found drugs on campuses across the country.

Major –The focal point of a student's college studies; a specific topic that is studied for a degree. Examples of majors include physics, English, history, computer science, economics, business, and music. Many students decide on a specific major before arriving on campus, while others are simply "undecided" until delcaring a major. Those who are extremely interested in two areas can also choose to double major.

Meal Block – The equivalent of one meal. Students on a meal plan usually receive a fixed number of meals per week. Each meal, or "block," can be redeemed at the school's dining facilities in place of cash. Often, a student's weekly allotment of meal blocks will be forfeited if not used.

Minor – An additional focal point in a student's education. Often serving as a complement or addition to a student's main area of focus, a minor has fewer requirements and prerequisites to fulfill than a major. Minors are not required for graduation from most schools; however some students who want to explore many different interests choose to pursue both a major and a minor.

Mushrooms – An illegal drug. Also known as "'shrooms," this drug resembles regular mushrooms but is extremely hallucinogenic.

Off-Campus Housing – Housing from a particular landlord or rental group that is not affiliated with the university. Depending on the college, off-campus housing can range from extremely popular to non-existent. Students who choose to live off campus are typically given more freedom, but they also have to deal with possible subletting scenarios, furniture, bills, and other issues. In addition to these factors, rental prices and distance often affect a student's decision to move off campus.

Office Hours – Time that teachers set aside for students who have questions about coursework. Office hours are a good forum for students to go over any problems and to show interest in the subject material.

Pledging – The early phase of joining a fraternity or sorority, pledging takes place after a student has gone through rush and received a bid. Pledging usually lasts between one and two semesters. Once the pledging period is complete and a particular student has done everything that is required to become a member, that student is considered a brother or sister. If a fraternity or a sorority would decide to "haze" a group of students, this initiation would take place during the pledging period.

Private Institution – A school that does not use tax revenue to subsidize education costs. Private schools typically cost more than public schools and are usually smaller.

Prof – Slang for "professor."

Public Institution – A school that uses tax revenue to subsidize education costs. Public schools are often a good value for in-state residents and tend to be larger than most private colleges.

Quarter System (or Trimester System) – A type of academic calendar system. In this setup, students take classes for three academic periods. The first quarter usually starts in late September or early October and concludes right before Christmas. The second quarter usually starts around early to mid–January and finishes up around March or April. The last academic quarter, or "third quarter," usually starts in late March or early April and finishes up in late May or Mid-June. The fourth quarter is summer. The major difference between the quarter system and semester system is that students take more, less comprehensive courses under the quarter calendar.

RA (Resident Assistant) – A student leader who is assigned to a particular floor in a dormitory in order to help to the other students who live there. An RA's duties include ensuring student safety and providing assistance wherever possible.

Recitation – An extension of a specific course; a review session. Some classes, particularly large lectures, are supplemented with mandatory recitation sessions that provide a relatively personal class setting.

Rolling Admissions – A form of admissions. Most commonly found at public institutions, schools with this type of policy continue to accept students throughout the year until their class sizes are met. For example, some schools begin accepting students as early as December and will continue to do so until April or May.

Room and Board – This figure is typically the combined cost of a university-owned room and a meal plan.

Room Draw/Housing Lottery – A common way to pick on-campus room assignments for the following year. If a student decides to remain in university-owned housing, he or she is assigned a unique number that, along with seniority, is used to determine his or her housing for the next year.

Rush – The period in which students can meet the brothers and sisters of a particular chapter and find out if a given fraternity or sorority is right for them. Rushing a fraternity or a sorority is not a requirement at any school. The goal of rush is to give students who are serious about pledging a feel for what to expect.

Semester System – The most common type of academic calendar system at college campuses. This setup typically includes two semesters in a given school year. The fall semester starts around the end of August or early September and concludes before winter vacation. The spring semester usually starts in mid-January and ends in late April or May.

Student Center/Rec Center/Student Union – A common area on campus that often contains study areas, recreation facilities, and eateries. This building is often a good place to meet up with fellow students; depending on the school, the student center can have a huge role or a non-existent role in campus life.

Student ID – A university-issued photo ID that serves as a student's key to school-related functions. Some schools require students to show these cards in order to get into dorms, libraries, cafeterias, and other facilities. In addition to storing meal plan information, in some cases, a student ID can actually work as a debit card and allow students to purchase things from bookstores or local shops.

Suite – A type of dorm room. Unlike dorms that feature communal bathrooms shared by the entire floor, suites offer bathrooms shared only among the suite. Suite-style dorm rooms can house anywhere from two to ten students.

TA (Teacher's Assistant) – An undergraduate or grad student who helps in some manner with a specific course. In some cases, a TA will teach a class, assist a professor, grade assignments, or conduct office hours.

Undergraduate – A student in the process of studying for his or her bachelor's degree.

ABOUT THE AUTHOR

Ian Spiro received a Bachelor of Science in Computer Science at Stanford University. He intends to take that Bachelor of Science, put it in a paper shredder, pulp it in a paper-grinder, and recycle it into the most beautiful resume-paper the world has ever seen. Ian expects to spend the first few years out of college in the serving industry and "just doing the right thing." After that, he plans to marry well and retire into a life of raising children and writing unpopular shareware programs. On the side, he might travel to Germany, or create freelance Internet comics.

Ian would like to thank his dedicated bounce-back team for their service in reading over the manuscript. He would also like to thank all the people who provided quotes, as well as the College Prowler management team, for continually reminding him that his deadline had passed.

Ian Spiro
ianspiro@collegeprowler.com

Notes

....

....

....

....

....

....

....

....

....

....

....

....

....

Notes

....

....

....

....

....

....

....

....

....

....

....

....

....

Notes

....

....

....

....

....

....

....

....

....

....

....

....

....

....

Notes

Notes

....

....

....

....

....

....

....

....

....

....

....

....

....

....

Notes

....

....

....

....

....

....

....

....

....

....

....

....

....

....

Notes

....

....

....

....

....

....

....

....

....

....

....

....

....

Notes

....

....

....

....

....

....

....

....

....

....

....

....

....

Need More Help?

Do you have more questions about this school? Can't find a certain statistic? College Prowler is here to help. We are the best source of college information on the planet. We have a network of thousands of students who can get the latest information on any school to you ASAP. E-mail us at info@collegeprowler.com with your college-related questions. It's like having an older sibling show you the ropes!

E-mail Us Your College-Related Questions!

Check out ***www.collegeprowler.com*** for more details.
1-800-290-2682

Notes

....

....

....

....

....

....

....

....

....

....

....

....

....

....

Tell Us What Life is Really Like at Your School!

Have you ever wanted to let people know what your school is really like? Now's your chance to help millions of high school students choose the right school.

Let your voice be heard and win cash and prizes!

Check out ***www.collegeprowler.com*** for more info!

Notes

....

....

....

....

....

....

....

....

....

....

....

....

....